KEIR HARDIE'S CREED

KEIR HARDIE'S CREED
Faith in Socialism

NEIL JOHNSON

WIPF & STOCK · Eugene, Oregon

Wipf & Stock
An Imprint of Wipf and Stock Publishers
199 W. 8th Ave., Suite 3
Eugene, OR 97401

www.wipfandstock.com

PAPERBACK ISBN: 978-1-6667-8069-7
HARDCOVER ISBN: 978-1-6667-8070-3
EBOOK ISBN: 978-1-6667-8071-0

VERSION NUMBER 10/23/23

Unless otherwise indicated, Scripture quotations are from the New Revised
Standard Version Bible: Anglicized Edition, copyright © 1989, 1995 Na-
tional Council of the Churches of Christ in the United States of America.
Used by permission. All rights reserved worldwide.

The Scripture quotation marked KJV is from the King James Version (London: Cambridge University Press, n.d.).

Dedicated to my Mam and Dad,
Joan and Bob Johnson

Contents

Preface

L ABOUR HISTORY is religious history. The story of the struggle of laboring people for social justice has been overwhelmingly underpinned by faith in the holiness of life. Throughout the centuries and worldwide, working people have found insight and inspiration from their faith in what they consider sacred. While the origins of the world faiths were about the pursuit of greater understanding and freedom, there is no denying that ideologies that were meant to liberate have been manipulated to oppress and enslave individuals and societies at critical points in history. But it is often at those critical moments that many people return to the core message of their religion to counter the injustices being imposed in its name. To focus on British history, the appeal to theological visions and principles is seen in the Peasants' Revolt, the English Revolution, early Methodism, the Chartists, and the birth of the labour movement. Throughout the twentieth century, faith continued to compel people to struggle for equality, freedom, and peace in the face of fascism, Soviet communism, and neoliberal capitalism. In an article that draws parallels with socialist and faith values, Dawn Foster wrote in the British journal *Tribune*,

> The poor of the world remain overwhelmingly believers,
> even as more elite layers become increasingly secular. . . .
> A left that is incapable of communicating with Christians
> and other people of faith will always be exclusive. As we
> seek to build broad alliances in favour of a new social

order in the coming years, we will find many believers in our ranks. They will be people who work against poverty, for unionisation, and the rights of workers, and are as worthy as any atheists as organisers of the Left.1

In the pursuit of greater equality, freedom, and peace for all people, the contemporary Labour movement must be fully inclusive as it seeks to celebrate and empower social, cultural, gender, sexual, and religious diversity. To do so means the movement must acknowledge that Labour politics is a sacred cause for many of its activists.

Neil Johnson
Birmingham, UK
June 2023

1. Foster, "Love Thy Neighbour," 63.

Acknowledgments

WITH THANKS TO Inderjit Bhogal, Sandra Jenkinson, and Hugh McLeod, for casting their expert eyes over an early draft of this manuscript.

Introduction

Labour's Prophetic Pioneer

Mr. Keir Hardie is undoubtedly an earnest social reformer. We wish him all success in his efforts to raise
the workers and procure for them a just share of the
produce of their labour. Some of his methods may be
questionable without affecting his sincerity. If we all
saw eye to eye there would be no problems to settle.
What we object to is the fond imagination that any
light upon the labour question, or any actual social
problem, can be found in the teachings of Christ.[1]

THE EARNEST SOCIAL REFORMER in question is James Keir
Hardie, a British Labour pioneer, who was both the first
independent working-class member of parliament and the first
leader of the nation's Labour Party. This attack on Keir Hardie's
creed comes from another earnest social reformer, G. W. Foote,
founder of the secularist journal *The Freethinker*. The article from
which the quotation is extracted responds to an interview published in the *Christian Commonwealth* where Hardie had spoken
about his Christian faith. Foote notes that at no point in the interview does Hardie express his belief in what Foote describes as

---

1. Foote, *Flowers of Freethought*, 165.

1

"the supernatural part of the Gospels."[2] From this observation, the secularist commentator asks, "Does he accept the New Testament miracles? Does he embrace the Incarnation and Resurrection? If he does, he is a Christian. If he does not, he has no right to call himself a Christian."[3] Foote was not alone in raising questions about Hardie's faith; others included leading figures within many mainstream Christian denominations across the English-speaking world. Yet, Hardie claimed to be faithful to the Christian gospel, and that his faith and politics were fused into one radically passionate ideology. This book is the first in-depth exploration of Keir Hardie's creed, a detailed study of his canon of beliefs, which was more concerned about realizing the essential core of Christianity than merely being a ticklist of doctrines. What unfurls is a truer grasp of Keir Hardie's religious socialism than previous studies have provided, an understanding that leads to questions for those on the political left today about their faith heritage, affiliations, and affinities.

The Theo-Political Context

The story of nineteenth-century Britain is the tale of industrialization, a revolution that was "gradual and relative in its impact."[4] Changes to the means of production, underpinned by capitalist control, which emerged in the late 1700s from the mills of Derbyshire and workshops of Birmingham, led to the complete upheaval of British society. A consistent and growing issue throughout this period was the "social question" or "labour question," the crux of it being how a rising working class, which provided the workforce upon which industrial society depended, should be regarded socially and represented politically. In the aftermath of the Napoleonic Wars, the campaign for political reform grew in strength across Britain as it tapped into grassroots unrest

2. Foote, *Flowers of Freethought*, 164.
3. Foote, *Flowers of Freethought*, 164.
4. Harvie and Matthew, *Nineteenth-Century Britain*, 1.

and dissent. By the 1830s one significant focus of the campaign's energy was Chartism. Taking their name from the People's Charter of 1838, the Chartists sought a greater democratization of the political system through a broadening of the voting franchise, secret ballots, paid members of parliament, equal constituencies, and annual parliamentary elections.

After twenty years of false hope for social and political recognition, Chartism became a spent force. The demise of the Chartist cause led to the movement for working-class political representation aligning with the radical reforming wing of the Liberal Party through alliances with national trade unions. A degree of political reform was achieved with the Representation of the People Act (Reform Act) of 1867, legislation that enfranchised part of the urban, male working-class (householders and lodgers paying rent of ten pounds or more each year) in England and Wales. This Reform Act made working men the majority of the electorate for the first time and opened the way for these new members of the electorate to stand for election to parliament. Working-class support for the Liberals culminated in the four premierships of William Ewart Gladstone between 1868 and 1894, a period when several trade unionists served as "Lib-Lab" MPs representing labor interests as members of the Liberal Party.

At the beginning of the nineteenth century around 20 percent of the population lived in urban areas; this reached 50 percent by the 1850s. Industrial towns and cities were growing so rapidly that housing was being built hastily, which could mean insubstantial provision, including appalling sanitary conditions. Initially, the working environment within factories, mills, and mines was not regulated, leading to dangerous conditions for the men, women, and children employed as manual laborers. Throughout the century, driven by social campaigns and movements, a series of parliamentary acts were passed that improved the working contexts of the laboring population. Similarly, after the Representation of the People Act of 1832, several long-fought campaigns for further reform acts gained parliamentary approval every few decades, enabling wider suffrage, though not all working men and no women of any social class had the vote by the end of the century. Internationally, this was a period of one hundred years of British imperial expansion through Canada, Australia, South Africa, India, and then across the African continent. By 1900 the British Empire was in control of one-fifth of the world's land and one-quarter of the global population.

A traditional religiosity remained within British society during this time, with Christianity giving a cultural context to the life of the nation.[5] In Scotland, the churches played a significant role in society, with Sunday attendance remaining relatively high by the end of the century compared to the figures for England. As well as contributing to the cultural identity of the Scottish people, whether that be through the Calvinism of the Church of Scotland and other Protestant denominations or Catholicism for the Irish-Scottish community, churches were pivotal in the provision of poor relief and basic education. Religious sectarianism was a major social and political issue, leading to hesitancy among Scottish churches to align themselves with any particular reforming movement, including Chartism, which gained a foothold in the political scene of Scotland during the 1820s and 1830s. The Scottish churches tried to avoid further divisions by claiming to represent the whole of a local community or parish rather than speaking for a certain social group or class.[6] It would not be until the end of the nineteenth century that the Christian denominations of Scotland began to make policy decisions based on the desire for social reform. Born and raised in that setting, Keir Hardie became a cause for change for both the political and religious institutions of his nation, be that Scotland or Britain, and across the wider empire.

A Brief Overview of the Life of Keir Hardie

The man who became known as James Keir Hardie was born on August 15, 1856, to a single mother called Mary Keir in

5. N. Johnson, *Labour Church*, 24.
6. Knox, "Religion and Scottish Labour," 613.

Legbrannock, North Lanarkshire, Scotland. Three years later, his mother married David Hardie, a ship carpenter. Hardie's earliest biographers do not refer to his illegitimacy, to the extent that some of these writers imply that his stepfather was his biological father. Later writers have speculated about the identity of the biological father, and whether the stigma of being illegitimate shaped Keir Hardie's personality and perspective on life. What has been emphasized throughout many of the biographies, from the first studies to recent works, is that his upbringing was nonreligious. The meaning of "nonreligious" has been interpreted in several ways, ranging from ardent atheism to freethinking, but the reality was more likely to be that organized religion was irrelevant to the daily struggles of the Hardie household. But when the Christian community offered practical support, the family was willing to benefit, so Keir received basic tuition from a church minister called Dan Craig. In later life, Keir Hardie recalled an incident relating to one of his first paid jobs, when at the age of ten he secured the position of delivery boy for a local Christian baker. His employment was cut short by the pious businessman, who had the young Keir wait until family prayers were concluded before sacking him for his lateness to work—Hardie would reflect that such behavior "makes me doubt the sincerity of those who make pretence in their prayers."[7] This statement expressed his relationship with an overtly pious form of Christianity that contrasted with Hardie's understating of the core message and contemporary application of the gospel of Jesus.

In response to her husband's conduct, Keir Hardie's mother encouraged her son to become an active member of the temperance movement through the Good Templars society. His involvement ironically led to his marriage to a publican's daughter, Lillie Wilson.[8] In 1864 Hardie was employed as a message boy for the Anchor Line Steamship Company, then two years later he became a pit trapper at Newarthill Colliery and began attending a night school to improve on his basic education. By 1879 Hardie had

7. Holman, *Keir Hardie*, 17–16.

8. Hughes, *Keir Hardie*, 27.

secured his first trade union role as a miners' agent. The previous year Hardie had embraced the Christian faith, nurtured by those he had encountered through the temperance movement, and then he and Lillie became members of the Cumnock Congregational Church in 1882. Hardie began to preach in local churches and helped to establish an Evangelical Union congregation with Rev. Andrew Scott following a dispute with the local church leadership over the pastoral and social needs of working families.[9]

In 1886 Keir Hardie was appointed as the secretary of the Scottish Miners' Federation. The following year, Hardie began publishing a monthly newspaper called *The Miner*. After associating with the Liberal Party, Hardie concluded that the working class needed their own political party, so he decided to stand for parliament in the Mid Lanarkshire by-election as an independent Labour candidate on April 27, 1888. He received the fewest votes in the poll. Later that year, on August 25, Hardie became a cofounder of the Scottish Labour Party and was elected secretary. At this time *The Miner* was relaunched under the title *Labour Leader*. Along with two other independent Labour candidates, Keir Hardie was successful in being elected to the London parliamentary seat of West Ham South in 1892 and entered the House of Commons in style, wearing a tweed suit and peaked cap. In October of that year, he addressed the Congress of the Congregational Union and accused the church of turning its back on the lives of working-class people. Such was the angry response from the congress members to his comments that he was forced to leave the platform.[10] The following January, Hardie presided over the founding conference of the Independent Labour Party (ILP) in Bradford, which was followed by an act of religious worship led by Rev. John Trevor of the Labour Church movement.[11] Keir Hardie was a leading advocate of the Labour Church, which promoted theological socialism, that "God was in the Labour Movement."[12]

9. Benn, *Keir Hardie*, 34.
10. "Mr Keir Hardie MP."
11. N. Johnson, *Labour Church*, 110.
12. Trevor, *Labour Church Hymn Book*, 2.

When his appeal for parliament to express condolences to the families of the 251 miners killed in a colliery explosion near Pontypridd in 1894 was refused because the business of the House of Commons that day was to mark the birth of a new royal baby, Hardie delivered a speech extremely critical of the monarchy. From his maiden speech onwards, Keir Hardie gained a reputation within and beyond parliament for being the MP who represented the poorest and most vulnerable members of society, most of whom had no vote. The loss of his parliamentary seat, along with the other twenty-seven ILP candidates, at the general election of 1895 was a hard blow to the British Labour movement. The ILP's hope had been built on the modest, though significant, electoral breakthrough of 1892, but an alliance in 1895 between the Conservative Party and the Liberal Unionist Party gained a large majority on an anti-Irish Home Rule ticket, while the ILP supported the cause of Home Rule.[13] Although outside of parliament, Keir Hardie remained a vital force in British politics during this time. In 1899 he was responsible for a motion to the Trade Union Congress proposing the formation of a distinct Labour group in the Houses of Parliament. Its success led to the establishment of the Labour Representative Committee (LRC), which acted as the means of convening and coordinating the MPs representing the interests of the British Labour movement, including the ILP, Social Democratic Federation, Fabian Society, and those parliamentarians sponsored by trade unions.

It was in 1899 that Hardie drew attention to John Campbell White, who became Lord Overtoun, the owner of several chemical works across Scotland. Overtoun was an overtly public Christian who promoted evangelical causes but was responsible for factories that poisoned their workers with their unregulated practices.[14] The

13. The Liberal Unionist Party was formed in 1886 as a breakaway anti-Irish Home Rule faction of the Liberal Party. The coalition with the Conservative Party led a decade of Unionist government between 1895 and 1905. A total merger of both political parties occurred in 1912.

14. "Lord Overtoun." Former Labour Party leader Gordon Brown retells a story told by his church minister father: "When he died one of his employees, disabled as a result of an accident due to the poor conditions in the Overtoun

force of Keir Hardie's attack on Lord Overtoun was reminiscent of his response to the treatment by his boyhood employer. Hardie's argument with both men was not simply about hypocrisy, because the baker and Overtoun were known to be diligent doctrinal list-tickers, the type expected of Christians by the secularist G. W. Foote; rather, for Keir Hardie their devotion was misdirected. Instead, Hardie's faith in Christianity was about a vision of transforming the world so that all people could live fully and freely, and that meant Christians were compelled to address the issues impacting the most oppressed people of every society.

Hardie won the Merthyr Tydfil and Aberdare seat for Labour in 1900; he was one of the two successful LRC candidates of the fifteen who stood for election. Though a small victory, this general election proved to be a turning point in the parliamentary campaigns for the British Labour movement. In June 1905, Hardie published an open letter to all members of the clergy challenging them to openly and overtly support his Unemployment Bill, which was being discussed in the House of Commons.[15] The issue was an unemployment crisis, so he used his open letter to challenge what he considered to be the prevalent pseudo-Christianity of the mainstream denominations by reiterating the key demands for justice from the gospel of Jesus of Nazareth. By 1906, the LRC had twenty-nine seats in the House of Commons, and it formally adopted the name "The Labour Party," with the ILP becoming an affiliated body. Hardie was appointed as the first leader of the parliamentary Labour Party.

Throughout the early 1900s, Hardie became increasingly associated with both women's suffrage and home rule for British colonies, often in opposition to official Labour Party policy. His reelection to his parliamentary seat was helped by growing support among the local nonconformist ministers, while nationally he became associated with the New Theology movement led by R. J.

---

chemical plant, walked around Glasgow with a placard saying 'Consternation in heaven: Lord Overtoun three days dead and not yet arrived" (Holman, *Keir Hardie*, 4).

15. Hardie, "Open Letter to Clergy."

Campbell, which linked Christian social concern with Labour politics.[16] Keir Hardie's politics and persona appealed to many within British nonconformist Christianity, whether they were Methodist, Baptist, Congregational, or independent, because he seemed to epitomize the spirit of dissent within which their faithful lives were held. Between 1907 and 1908 Hardie toured parts of the British Empire, visiting India, Australasia, and South Africa, taking great interest in their different social and religious customs and beliefs. Due to ill health, Hardie resigned as Labour Party leader in January 1908, then dedicated his time to the campaign for women's suffrage and pacifist causes. In June 1910, Hardie addressed a large socialist rally in the northern French city of Lille when he spoke to his European comrades about the socialism of Jesus Christ.[17] As a committed pacifist, Hardie despaired at the outbreak of the First World War on August 4, 1914. After several years of declining health, James Keir Hardie died on September 26, 1915.

Biographical Portrayals

During the past century, there has been a plethora of biographies written about James Keir Hardie. Initially, the output came from the pens of comrades and friends, who reflected on the campaigns and conversations they had shared with Hardie. In time biographers became politicians and historians, who often recruited their subject to their own causes through the retelling of his life story. The centenary year of Hardie's death in 2015 generated renewed consideration about his contribution to British Labour history and politics, as well as his relevance to the contemporary political and social scene.[18] What is consistent throughout the biographical works is the view that Keir Hardie was a pioneer in British working-class politics as he broke the ties with the Liberal Party, and he had been the founding father of the Parliamentary Labour

16. Benn, *Keir Hardie*, 205.

17. "Keir Hardie on Continent."

18. Working Class Movement's Library, "Keir Hardie Centenary Conference."

Party. Beyond the mantle of pioneer and founder, many biographers have viewed Hardie as a person and political leader through a particularly religious lens.

Within two years of Hardie's death, a Canadian socialist, J. McArthur Conner, had a short biography published about the British Labour leader. Canada in 1917 was witnessing the stirrings of a social gospel movement, which would ignite during the General Strike in 1919 and lead to significant changes in the political and church life of the nation. McArthur Conner writes of Hardie, "The world knew him as a fighter, an agitator, a Socialist,"[19] and continues with a bold statement:

> Since the days of Christ till Hardie came upon the scene there had not been anyone who from both the religious and economic standpoint fought the battle of the oppressed and downtrodden as he did. Truly he was the voice in the wilderness preparing the way and making the paths straight for general economic justice.[20]

Keir Hardie, the latter-day John the Baptist, was but one of many religious portrayals of the man as his political legacy was claimed and constantly refashioned over the years. A Memorial Committee was formed to commission an authorized biography of Hardie, originally to be written by his Scottish socialist comrade, John Bruce Glasier, who had produced a memorial booklet to mark his death in 1915. But with Glasier's ill health, then his death in 1920, the task passed to another comrade and biographer of Robert Burns, William Stewart. Keir Hardie's significance is described by Stewart as "one of the permanently historic figures in that great age-long progressive movement which must find its complete realization in the establishment of human equality on a basis of mutual service by all members of the human family."[21] The book's introductory chapter was written by James Ramsay MacDonald, one of the early members of the Parliamentary Labour

---

19. McArthur Conner, *Jas. Keir Hardie*, 3.
20. McArthur Conner, *Jas. Keir Hardie*, 22.
21. Stewart, *J. Keir Hardie*, 374.

Party alongside Hardie and leader of the party from 1922. Here
Hardie's place in history is sanctified:

> His whole being lay under the shadow of the hand of
> the crowned Authority which told him of its presence
> now by a lightning flash, now by a whisper, and now by
> a mere tremor in his soul like what the old folk believed
> went through the earth when night died, and the day was
> born. The world was life, not things, to him.[22]

Most of Keir Hardie's biographers have been sympathetic to
the man and his cause, and some could be described as devotees
or disciples. But even the more critical biographies acknowledge
Hardie's role as a groundbreaking figure in Labour politics, both
for Britain and internationally. Some of the devotees and critics
adopted religious terms to define the contribution and importance
of the man and his message. During the past hundred years or so,
James Keir Hardie has been called an evangelist,[23] a prophet,[24] a
mystic,[25] a visionary,[26] a "touchstone of civilization,"[27] Christlike,[28]
and "an Old Testament figure,"[29] who was worthy of canoniza-
tion as a revolutionary,[30] though more recent commentators have
warned against the danger of "patronising dismissal"[31] through
socialist sainthood. While few recent biographers painted him as a
saint, those who view Hardie through a religious lens have tended
to settle on the portrayal of a prophetic figure, someone who spoke
with divine authority about the eternal values of peace, justice, and
equality, and offered a warning to those who used their power to

22. Stewart, *J. Keir Hardie*, xxiii.
23. F. Johnson, *Keir Hardie's Socialism*, 7.
24. Maxton, *Keir Hardie*, 14.
25. Fyfe, *Keir Hardie*, 62.
26. F. Williams, *Fifty Years' March*, 85.
27. Morgan, *Labour People*, 38.
28. Holman, *Keir Hardie*, 203.
29. Pugh, *Speak For Britain!*, 24.
30. Hill, "Keir Hardie," 172.
31. Howell, "Hunting for the Real."

deny or stymie the privileges and principles meant for the whole of humanity.

Recognizing a Socialist Christian

> Hardie's Socialism can neither be classified as scientific or Utopian. . . . So far as he was influenced towards Socialism by the ideas of others, it was as he stated, by the Bible, the songs of Burns, the writings of Carlyle, Ruskin, and Mill, and the democratic tradition in the working-class homes in Scotland in his early days. In the main, however, as with many of us, he derived his Socialism from his thought and feeling, the plight of the workers, and the state of the world.[32]

Written shortly after Hardie's death in a memorial booklet, these are the words of John Bruce Glasier, who followed Hardie as editor of *Labour Leader*. These few sentences offer us a sense of the ideological influences upon Keir Hardie's political philosophy and personal beliefs. From his earliest years, Hardie was intrigued, inspired, and instigated by numerous founts of insight. His family upbringing meant that when Hardie began to engage with the dissenting Christian culture of chapel life and faith it was done so with a grounding in other sources, including the radical Romanticism of Robert Burns, and an openness to those regarded as freethinkers of the eighteenth and nineteenth centuries, mainly from Britain, but increasingly from Europe and beyond.

Keir Hardie has been frequently branded as a Christian socialist. Based on that labeling, Hardie is viewed and interpreted as part of a tradition that, in its most formalized British expression, can be traced back to the mid-nineteenth-century Anglican theologian and social commentator F. D. Maurice, who argued that Christianity offered the basis to the transformation of society in an age of industrial-scale injustice. In his doctoral thesis "Christian Socialism as Political Ideology," Anthony Williams argues that from Maurice onwards, for British Christian socialists

32. Glasier, *Keir Hardie*, 10.

"it was the Christian religion which was above all else the basis for their socialism. Christian Socialists looked to the Bible, arguing that it showed through the Fatherhood of God that all men were brothers."[33] Williams acknowledges that those "tagged with the label 'Christian Socialist' do not here constitute a homogenous bloc"; he goes on to state, "They all make reference to the Fatherhood of God, the brotherhood of man, the teaching and example of Christ, and the teaching of the church throughout the ages."[34]

If the fatherhood of God and the brotherhood of man are pivotal beliefs to Christian socialism, then Keir Hardie cannot be classified as belonging to that tradition. There is little trace of reference to the fatherhood of God in speeches, articles, and books delivered and written throughout his career. Some of Hardie's biographers have questioned the impact of his illegitimacy on his life and outlook,[35] and so it could follow that he was not able to relate fully to the concept of God as Father. When compared to other contemporary British socialists and Labour activists who claimed a Christian foundation to their politics, Hardie is not alone in the lack of emphasis on divine fatherhood. During Labour Week (May 1–8) 1910, Keir Hardie was among ten male speakers to address a series of meetings at Browning Hall in Walworth, London, on the subject of "Labour and Religion." Half of the Labour politicians referred to God in their homilies, including the present and future leaders of the Labour Party Arthur Henderson and George Lansbury, while the other five, such as the first Labour Chancellor of the Exchequer (Philip Snowden) and Keir Hardie, spoke of religion in terms of a moral code which bore the name of Jesus.[36] This raises the issue of whether Williams's doctrinal definition of Christian socialism is accurate, or should another term be found to define the religious politics of figures like Hardie?

In my study of the Labour Church movement, I made a distinction between Christian socialists and socialist Christians,

33. A. Williams, "Christian Socialism," 113.
34. A. Williams, "Christian Socialism," 115.
35. Holman, *Keir Hardie*, 24.
36. See Ten Labour Members, *Labour and Religion*.

arguing that Christian socialists saw in socialism the means of applying Christian principles to social issues, while socialist Christians discovered values in socialism that had been lost to the church, making their politics bring relevance to the teaching of Jesus Christ for contemporary society. The clearest distinction was their relationship to the traditional Christian denominations and affiliation to their creeds. Christian socialists remained within the membership of the Christian church and then proclaimed their politics from that position, but socialist Christians spoke from outside of institutional Christianity.[37] During my research into the Labour Church and its political and theological context, I came across many late-Victorian British socialists who claimed Jesus of Nazareth as a prophet of their cause, even though they had rejected certain creedal aspects of Christianity. Some talked about the "religion of socialism" as a means of explaining their conviction to a political cause that offered a vision to them of heaven on earth.[38] What unites the socialist Christians and Christian socialists is the Christocentricity of their beliefs. I agree with W. W. Knox, that "Socialist Christianity was encapsulated in the figure of Keir Hardie,"[39] because his theology was Christocentric, and that the nature, will, and ways of the divine were revealed and realized in the figure of Jesus. From his early days in the Evangelical Union and throughout his life in the Labour movement, when Hardie spoke about God he did so in terms of encounter through positive, affirming, and creative relationships. This relational concept of divinity led to his creed of the sacred kinship promoted through socialism, a "creed of fraternity and equality."[40]

---

37. N. Johnson, *Labour Church*, 27.

38. See Conway and Glasier, *Religion of Socialism*.

39. Knox, "Religion and Scottish Labour," 609.

40. Cruddas, "Keir Hardie's Ethical Socialism," 16.

Institutional Christian Reactions

When Keir Hardie died in 1915 there were many heartfelt, sorrow-ful tributes from some leading church figures of various denomina-tions and traditions. These tributes express a growing appreciation of Hardie's vision and commitments from among both local and national religious leaders. But in his early political career, and to a certain extent throughout his public life, Keir Hardie was a target for official Christians across Britain to attack the principles of his socialism. In so far as he symbolized, even personified, the Labour cause in Britain for almost thirty years, the change in attitude to Hardie by leading Christians over the years is an indication of a shift in views to how the "labour question" could be answered po-litically and religiously.

In an article published in March 1894, the Old Testament scholar Rev. Dr. Robert A. Watson took aim at the socialism proclaimed by Keir Hardie, arguing that it offered false hope to the suffering masses and was creeping into the life of the British churches.

> Suppose that matters are as Mr. Hardie says, and that individuals do gain at the expense of the community. The way of freedom, the way of life, is not to make this impossible economically, but to prevent it through the operation of a spiritual law. Here, if nowhere else, Chris-tianity and Socialism are at dagger drawn.[41]

Watson's point is that the purpose of Christian mission in late-Victorian society was not about promoting wishful utopia-nism, but the conversion of the capitalist so that he would share his wealth with his poor neighbor. Christ is primarily concerned with the liberation of the human soul, something that the gospel of socialism ignored, Watson argues. Hardie's opposition to the hypocrisy of chemical works owner Lord Overtoun in 1899 stirred up comments from those who wished to defend the pious Chris-tian capitalist. A reference to the otherworldly emphasis of the apostle Paul's theology of salvation in one of the numerous articles

---

41. Watson, "Keir Hardie on Socialism."

and pamphlets produced by Hardie to build his case against Overtoun was held up for criticism. For example, Congregational minister Rev. T. W. Hodge of Newport stated it was ludicrous "that an agitator of the nineteenth century should stand in judgment on the great Apostle. Paul had done more for working men than Keir Hardie had ever done, or was likely to do."[42] Watson and Hodge fit into a category of Christian critics of socialism, according to Anthony Williams, who stated that alongside moral and economic disagreements, their arguments are about the fundamental incompatibility between Christianity and socialist politics and offer a defense of private property and social order.[43]

But there were other church leaders for whom their Christian faith and socialism were natural allies. *Labour Leader* published a variety of responses from Anglican clergy in reply to Keir Hardie's "Open Letter" to them in 1905. One reply printed came from someone calling himself "A Durham Priest," who wrote, "We are Socialists because we are Churchmen, and resent the awful perversity which marks the Church of the Carpenter of Nazareth."[44] Rev. J. B. Hyde, the rector of Kirk Ireton, responds by arguing for a reformation of both methods and morals as the common cause: "Even among the clergy there are a few who preach the gospel of the Crucified Carpenter, and try in all ways to help those for whom He lived and died. These are also trying to make the crooked straight, and the rough smooth."[45]

In 1910, Wesleyan Methodist minister Rev. Harold Crawford Walters addressed his congregation in Bedford and stated that Christianity was responsible for the social movements of the day; the question was about the future relationship between faith and politics as the movements progressed.

> Some time ago Mr. Keir Hardie, one of the Socialist leaders, stated that it was his religion that had *led him to Socialism*, and Socialism and religion, when they were

42. "Lord Overtoun. Mr Lorimer."

43. A. Williams, "Christian Socialism," 238.

44. "A Durham Priest," in "Clergy and the ILP."

45. J. B. Hyde, in "Clergy and the ILP."

rightly understood and looked at from the highest possible standpoint, ought to work toward one common end
in one common army. He used the word Socialism not
as used by any particular party in this country, but as the
best term that came to hand for expressing the political
ideals of the kingdom of God.[46]

At the beginning of 1910 Keir Hardie was fighting for his parliamentary seat of Merthyr Tydfil at a general election. His campaign
that year has been described as a crusade because of the support
he received from a local network of religious leaders and their congregations.[47] Francis Williams in his history of the early Labour
Party wrote that Hardie was able to connect with those "whose
radicalism was linked closely with their staunch nonconformity."[48]

In response to the announcement of his death, two church
leaders and Christian socialists from different traditions paid tribute to Keir Hardie. R. J. Campbell said of him, "He was a truly great
man, and one of the most unselfish and single-minded men I have
ever known,"[49] while Canon J. G. Adderley, regarding the condemnation by some on religious grounds of Hardie and his politics,
paid homage to the Labour leader:

I doubt . . . there has been a closer mixture of religion and
politics in any one individual. He represented the exact
antithesis to the German Atheist Socialist. It was only the
gross blindness of many of his political opponents which
prevented them from seeing this and caused them to at-
tribute to him the infidel motives which they did. They
were the real infidels who would not believe that God
could work His will through the unorthodox. May God
give us a few more "Atheists" like Keir Hardie![50]

46. "Christianity and Twentieth Century" (emphasis original).
47. Benn, *Keir Hardie*, 257.
48. F. Williams, *Fifty Years' March*, 105.
49. Campbell, "Rev R J Campbell's Tribute."
50. "Keir Hardie's Religion."

Tracing Keir Hardie's Creed

With an understanding of the background and setting of Keir Hardie's life, and a sense of his political career, this study endeavors to trace both the influences upon and the elements of his creed. At the heart of Hardie's faith was the figure of Jesus, the worker from Nazareth and political agitator, who championed the cause of the poor and marginalized. How Keir Hardie viewed Jesus is considered in chapter 1 by recognizing the significance of Renan's *Life of Jesus*, and the later influence of R. J. Campbell's *The New Theology* upon his perspective. Ultimately, Hardie saw Jesus as a symbol of working-class struggle, with the incarnation being the ultimate event or demonstration of sacred solidarity. The gospel of Jesus was about an alternative world, the kingdom of God on earth, where there would be a total reordering of human relationships; this is the subject of chapter 2. Hardie interpreted the new world order of God's kingdom in terms of a sacred egalitarianism, a universal comradeship or kinship, which was the will of the divine for the whole of creation, including humankind.

While Jesus of Nazareth was central to his creed, Hardie understood him to be part of an ancient prophetic tradition that acted as a constant reminder of the nature and will of God. Chapter 3 explores Hardie's understanding of prophecy and practice in Judeo-Christian history. Keir Hardie appreciated the role of the Hebrew prophets as messengers, enactors, and symbols of divine presence and purpose. They held the people and their leaders to account by calling them to repent and renew their commitment to the sacred cause of justice, peace, and solidarity. The Christian communities of the early church demonstrated to Hardie prophecy in practice by their members living out the universal kinship and egalitarianism promised by the kingdom of God on earth, thus offering a practical model for wider society. Hardie referenced the first Christians as a sign of hope that the reordering of social relationships personified in Jesus, envisioned as the kingdom of God, and constantly proclaimed throughout the prophetic tradition was achievable with vision, will, and action. After the corruption of

Christianity through its adoption by the powers of the Roman Empire and its successors, Keir Hardie traced a radical movement that remained faithful to the gospel of God's new world revealed by Jesus of Nazareth, either in name or in spirit. By seeking a religion of humanity (the focus of chapter 4) Hardie found a common thread that acknowledged and celebrated the divine in human solidarity. From Robert Burns to contemporary social commentators, across the radical Christian history of Britain and Europe, and within the truths of world religious traditions, Hardie wove together ideologies that were not natural allies, yet they brought texture and heft to his creed.

Keir Hardie concluded that socialism was the Christianity of his day, the supreme expression of the overarching and interwoven universal religion that declares the divinity of human solidarity. Chapter 5 considers Hardie's socialism, which was an inclusive, "big tent" faith system that embraced the whole Labour movement, both nationally and internationally. The domestic and global dimensions of socialism are reflected in Keir Hardie's affinity with Karl Marx, whom he considered to be a prophet of the future, and with William Morris, a prophet who reminded the movement of its rich heritage from the past. Although he was open to the contributions and insights from his broad and diverse comrades across the international Labour movement, Hardie was committed to parliamentary democracy and so he struggled for an electoral mandate for the socialist cause, believing that would be the means of achieving a society based on a godly egalitarianism.

In the concluding chapter a summary of the book's research will be offered, reminding the reader of how the influences and elements of Keir Hardie's faith and politics have been traced. This is followed by a drafting out of Hardie's creed, a composite statement based on his speeches, newspaper articles, and other publications dating back to the 1890s, but mostly from the last ten years of his life, which offer both an overview and the maturity of his thought. Having considered the meaning of this creed, the question is raised about the relevance of the study for contemporary politics and faith. The challenge is addressed by unpacking some of the possible implications for today of the central theme of the book's thesis, that Keir Hardie's creed is a proclamation of solidarity, which he believed to be of paramount importance for the future of our world.

I

Jesus of Nazareth

The rich and comfortable classes had annexed Jesus and perverted his Gospel. And yet He belongs to the workers in a special degree, and the Brotherhood movement is tending to restore Jesus to His rightful place as the Friend and Saviour of the poor.[1]

BY INVITATION of the *Foyer du Peuple* (People's home) Protestant mission, Keir Hardie was a member of a "Pleasant Sunday Afternoon (PSA) Brotherhood of Workingmen" delegation to Lille in northern France for a rally on Pentecost Sunday, May 15, 1910. The PSA Brotherhood and Sisterhood movement was an ecumenical, nonconformist, social welfare organization, founded in 1875 by Congregationalist deacon John Blackham in the West Midlands town of West Bromwich. Emerging from the adult Bible class movement,[2] the PSA Brotherhood/Sisterhood played a role in forging links between local nonconformist and "low church" Anglican Christian communities with the British Labour movement. The leaders of *Foyer du Peuple* organized the Pentecost rally as part of a campaign to introduce the PSA movement to French

1. "Keir Hardie on Continent."
2. Killingray, "Pleasant Sunday Afternoon Movement," 262.

Protestants who were proclaiming the social gospel of Jesus Christ.[3] Accompanied by 260 PSA Brothers, Keir Hardie felt that he was at home among fellow socialist Christians, both British and French, to declare the kernel of his creed: "I myself have found in the Christianity of Christ the inspiration which first of all drove me into the Movement, and which has carried me on in it."[4]

Primarily, Keir Hardie's creed was Christ-centered, or more accurately, Jesus-focused. At the heart of his faith was Jesus of Nazareth, the child of a carpenter household in Galilee as portrayed by the Gospel writers in the New Testament. Former Labour Party leader Jeremy Corbyn wrote about the significance of Hardie's involvement in the life of the church and temperance movement to his formation as a private and public figure, which he argued was as important as Hardie's engagement within the trade union and labour movement.[5] The temperance movement promoted self-improvement from the position of a fundamental belief in the self-worth of humanity, and, in the case of the Independent Order of Good Templars to which Hardie belonged, campaigned for improved working, housing, and social conditions of working-class communities.[6] Through his membership in the local branch, Keir Hardie discovered that he shared the same values and aspirations with those whose primary motivation for activism was their Christian faith. The influence of Christian members upon this son of a nonreligious family drew him into a church community that upheld and advanced his views and understandings, which in turn led Hardie to a very personal faith, a faith in the person of Jesus.

> In these, the early days of his Trade-Union activity, he was not a Socialist; apart from his Trade-Union work his public interests were absorbed in temperance propaganda—he remained an abstainer to the day of his death—and in propaganda work on behalf of the Evangelical Union, or Morisonians, whose rejection of the sterner

---

3. Chalamet, *Revivalism and Social Christianity*, 32.
4. "Keir Hardie on Continent."
5. Corbyn, "Afterword," 183.
6. Nicholson, *Knights Templar*, 272.

doctrines of Calvinism and insistence upon the gospel
tenets of human salvation made a strong appeal to him.[7]

These words of Thomas Johnston, a Scottish socialist journalist-cum-politician and younger contemporary of Keir Hardie, lead us to a primary source of influence on Hardie's conception of Jesus, the Evangelical Union. Hardie experienced the union initially through the ministry of Reverend Andrew Scott and the congregation in Cumnock that they established together. The Evangelical Union was formed in 1843 under the leadership of Reverend James Morison, after the expulsion on the grounds of heresy of four ministers (including Morison and his father) from the Scottish United Secession Church.[8] Calvinism, which originated in the theology of the Protestant Reformer John Calvin, emphasized the depravity of humankind and the doctrine of predestination under the sovereignty of God. Predestination is the belief that God predetermines some people, an "elect," to be saved for eternity, while the rest of humanity is destined for eternal damnation.[9] In contrast, the Morisonian theological basis of the congregations associated with the Evangelical Union stressed the freedom of humanity due to the universality of God's gracious love expressed in Jesus Christ.[10] Morison placed particular significance on the incarnation of God through Jesus as the point when he attained his divine sonship, rather than Jesus Christ being the Son of God for all eternity;[11] in other words, it is through the event of sacred solidarity with humankind, the incarnation, that the relevance of Jesus is to be understood by every generation that followed him.

The concept of Jesus conveyed by the Morisonian Christology of the Evangelical Union was a very human, historical figure, who revealed through his life and ministry a godly egalitarianism. For

7. Tracey, *Book of Labour Party*, 107.

8. After numerous unifications, the United Secession Church would eventually become part of the Presbyterian Church of Scotland in 1929, while the Evangelical Union joined the Congregational Union of Scotland in 1896.

9. Calvin, *Institutes*, 2206.

10. Kirsch, "Theology of James Morison," 8.

11. Kirsch, "Theology of James Morison," 4.

someone like Keir Hardie who approached Christianity from the perspective of a growing social consciousness and political commitment, the portrayal of Jesus as an ordinary human being who identified with poor and marginalized people, and fought for their social justice, was extremely attractive to the point of utter reverence. James Morison's understanding of the incarnation as the event or demonstration of sacred solidarity with humankind was a pivotal insight for Hardie, as it shaped his concept of the nature and will of God. In the figure of Jesus, what is divine is revealed and realized by just and empowering relationships. Throughout his public career, Hardie referred to Jesus of Nazareth as a source of his socialist principles. A newspaper report from 1893 offers a sense of Keir Hardie's Jesus-focused politics:

> [Keir Hardie] wanted to see the democracy fully installed in power with a knowledge of the principles which underlie right-doing on the part of the people. These principles were concisely summed up in the teachings of Jesus of Nazareth. If the maxim about doing unto others as we would have them do unto us were to be the government of this country it would not be possible for the hideous iniquities which now prevailed to continue for twenty-four hours. Under the operation of Christian principles, everything else would have to stand aside until slumdom and sweating had been swept out of existence.[12]

Another insight into how Jesus of Nazareth was viewed is given by Hardie's article about the literature that had influenced his life in a 1906 edition of the cultural journal *Review of Reviews*. He cites various writers that he recalled from his childhood and later life, including the work of Robert Burns, which will be explored in a later chapter. The book through which Keir Hardie interpreted the biblical accounts of Jesus and the early church draws our attention to a particular perspective of Christianity's central figure.

> I have left out Burns' poems and the New Testament, which in a sense were always with me, especially the former; I had nearly reached man's estate before I read

12. "Mr Keir Hardie at Labour Church."

the [latter], nor did I appreciate it fully until I had read Renan's *Life of Jesus*.[13]

Joseph Ernest Renan was a French philosopher, biblical scholar, Semitic linguist, and historian of religion. While he was travelling through the Middle East, including parts of Palestine, in 1861 with his sister Henrietta, tragedy struck when Henrietta died suddenly after suffering from a fever. In the midst of his grief, and with the New Testament and a copy of the works of the first-century Roman historian Flavius Josephus as his only reference texts, Renan began writing *Vie de Jésus*, which would be published in 1863 in French, then later that year in an English edition. Condemned by certain Roman Catholic clerics in his own country, *The Life of Jesus* became a popular text for those wrestling with "crisis of faith" issues relating to evolutionary theories and critical biblical scholarship that questioned conventional Christian teaching.[14] Renan concentrated on the search for the historic Jesus as revealed in the Gospels, particularly the Gospel of John, which he justified by stating,

> Far removed from the simple, disinterested, impersonal tone of the Synoptics, the Gospel of John shows incessantly the pre-occupation of the apologist—the mental reservation of the sectarian, the desire to prove a thesis, and to convince adversaries.[15]

Renan's depiction of Jesus emphasizes his humanity, arguing that he instilled the Spirit of God, placing him alongside other historical figures who had changed how humanity viewed reality: "Jesus gave religion to humanity, as Socrates gave it philosophy, and Aristotle science."[16] Renan's Jesus goes beyond his Jewish identity and context: "Far from Jesus having continued Judaism, he represents the rupture from the Jewish spirit."[17] Such a distancing from

13. Hughes, *Keir Hardie's Speeches*, 138.

14. Gore, "Introduction," ix.

15. Renan, *Life of Jesus*, 15.

16. Renan, *Life of Jesus*, 236.

17. Renan, *Life of Jesus*, 242.

the religious, cultural, and racial roots of Jesus has been criticized by later commentators claiming that Renan's portrayal is of an Aryan Christ,[18] while others have written that this is a misreading of *Vie de Jésus* when placed alongside Renan's other work.[19] What is clear about the figure of Jesus in Renan's study is that he is non-dogmatic, very pragmatic, with a passionate social conscious: "Jesus was not a founder of dogmas, or a maker of creeds; he infused into the world a new spirit."[20] For Renan, Jesus was the greatest of human beings, and through the profound heights and depths of his humanity, the world was able to grasp a concept of the divine.

> But whatever may be the unexpected phenomena of the future, Jesus will not be surpassed. His worship will constantly renew its youth, the tale of his life will cause ceaseless tears, his sufferings will soften the best hearts; all the ages will proclaim that among the sons of men, there is none born who is greater than Jesus.[21]

The influence of Renan's portrayal of Jesus on Keir Hardie's thinking and faith is echoed in his writings and speeches throughout his public life. On Sunday, January 21, 1894, Keir Hardie addressed a rally in the Prince of Wales Theatre in Salford. The event had been organized by the Manchester and Salford Labour Church, which was part of the religiopolitical organization founded by Rev. John Trevor in 1891 based on the belief that "God was in the Labour Movement."[22] As noted in the introductory chapter, Hardie was an advocate of the Labour Church, and consequently, he became a popular speaker at services and events arranged by local Labour Church congregations across Britain. According to a newspaper report of the Salford rally, the topic of Keir Hardie's address was "The Gospel of Jesus Christ."

18. Heschel, *Aryan Jesus*, 34.

19. See Dagon, "Ernest Renan."

20. Renan, *Life of* Jesus, 236.

21. Renan, *Life of* Jesus, 244.

22. Trevor, *Labour Church Hymn Book*, 2.

He proposed to consider the Gospel of Jesus Christ from the standpoint of one man trying to read the life and history of another man. Jesus Christ, whom millions professed to worship, was, in His day and generation, an ordinary member of the working classes, the son of working-class parents, living the Life of the working classes of His day and generation. (Hear, hear.) Learned His trade as a joiner and carpenter like His father before Him, like any other working man of the community. Surely the influence of a working man, who had influenced the opinions of the whole of the Western world, was well worth inquiring into in this generation.[23]

The message of the address was for his hearers to consider the gospel of Jesus of Nazareth as the ordinary worker proclaiming human solidarity within the grace of God, compared with the contemporary Christian churches, which expressed a false gospel that justified the segregation of rich from poor. With regard to the question of why working people were no longer attending these churches, Hardie concluded his address, "Because for six days in the week, he [the worker] was oppressed, and on the Sunday, if he went to church, saw his oppressor exalted and himself debased."[24]

Eighteen years later, at the time of the national coal strike of 1912, the first national strike by coal miners in the country with over a million miners participating, Hardie spoke at an event in Cardiff. Led by the Miners' Federation of Great Britain, the main aim of the industrial action was to secure a minimum wage for those working in the coal mining sector. The ballot paper that triggered the strike read, "Are you in favour of giving notice to establish the principle of a minimum wage for every man and boy working underground in the mines of Great Britain?"[25] Eventually after thirty-seven days, H. H. Asquith's Liberal government intervened and ended the strike by passing the Coal Mines Act, which brought in a minimum wage for the first time. On the eve of the national coal strike a copy of a prayer was sent out to all

23. "Mr Hardie MP in Manchester."
24. "Mr Hardie MP in Manchester."
25. See Gill, "National Coal Strike."

congregations in the Church of England on behalf of its senior leaders, the archbishops of Canterbury and York:

> O God, Who art the Father of all, and Who alone makest man to be of one mind in a house, we beseech Thee, at this time of strife and unrest, to grant to us, by the inspiration of Thy Holy Spirit, a fuller realisation of our brotherhood man with man in Thee; allay all danger and bitterness, and deepen in us a sense of truth and equity in our dealings one with another, for the sake of Thy Son our Lord Jesus Christ, Amen.[26]

Keir Hardie's response to the strike also called upon the name of Jesus, but in more radical terms than the archbishops' prayer. The new spirit that Jesus infused into the world, according to Renan's biography of Jesus, was experienced in Hardie's words to his audience, as reported by the local press.

> Mr. Keir Hardie, speaking at Cardiff in connection with the religious and labour unrest last night, welcomed the opportunity of stating his conception of Jesus of Nazareth in relation to the modern democratic movement. Jesus was a working man and a public agitator and was executed as a revolutionary leader. The national life of his time was that of to-day on a smaller scale, materialism being its dominant feature. What Christianity was then Socialism was to-day, and the present coal strike was but the working of the spirit of God in the hearts of the men who felt existing wrong, and were striving to bring Christ's kingdom a little nearer.[27]

Several of Keir Hardie's biographers have commented on his self-identification with the figure of Jesus.[28] The image of the self-sacrificing worker pursuing justice through solidarity for the most marginalized of his society struck a chord with the politician who gained the nickname of "the Member of Parliament for the Unemployed" during the initial period of his national political life.

26. See Gill, "National Coal Strike."
27. "Mr Keir Hardie MP in Cardiff."
28. Reid, *Keir Hardie*, 44; Morgan, *Keir Hardie*, 193.

Hardie's religious formation within the Evangelical Union and his reading of Renan offered a perspective on the figure of Jesus of Nazareth that he would cite as the constant source of inspiration for his life, faith, and politics. Caroline Benn in her study of Keir Hardie takes Hardie's self-identification with Jesus to an intimate level with reference to his childhood:

> Hardie's personal circumstances [cannot] be altogether over-looked—even if the influence was unconscious—that he was born without a father to a mother called Mary, living with her own mother, who afterwards married a carpenter and had many more children. There is even the distorted attempt to give Hardie, when he turned out to be an extraordinary man, a mysterious and unusual pedigree, to complete the picture.[29]

Benn alludes to attempts, both during and after his lifetime, to associate Hardie with the figure of Jesus Christ. Kenneth O. Morgan notes at the beginning of his biography, "A Welsh admirer, Wil Jon Edwards, saw him as a messianic figure, a latter-day Jesus: 'he and his gospel were indivisible.'"[30] For another biographer, Bob Holman, Hardie identified himself with the suffering and death of Jesus throughout his life."[31]

From 1907 Keir Hardie became associated with New Theology by sharing a platform with Reverend R. J. Campbell, the Congregational minister of the City Temple in London, which was considered to be one of Britain's nonconformist "cathedrals." Like the other great dissenting chapels, including the Wesleyan Methodist Central Halls and Salvation Army Citadels, the City Temple was primarily a "preaching house" where people gathered to be challenged and inspired by the power of the oratory from its pulpit. While his predecessors (and most of his successors) were conservative in their theology, Reginald John Campbell proved himself to be radical in both faith and politics, which were fused together into his Sunday sermons. Such was the growing popularity of

29. Benn, *Keir Hardie*, 18.

30. Edwards, *From the Valley*, 11.

31. Holman, *Keir Hardie*, 204.

Campbell's message that his sermons were published in several volumes under the title of *The New Theology*, which he defined as "rationalised Christianity."[32] The Christology of Campbell's New Theology was based on the concept of "Jesus the Divine Man."[33]

> Jesus was Divine simply and solely because His life was never governed by any other principle. We do not need to talk of two natures in Him, or to think of a mysterious dividing line, on one side of which He was human, and on the other Divine. In Him humanity was Divinity, and Divinity humanity.[34]

This resonates with the Morisonian concept of incarnation as the demonstration or event of sacred solidarity with humanity, a bond revealed in Jesus, both as the person in history and as the symbol of the nature and will of the divine.

Just as Renan had called for a return to the historical Jesus of Nazareth to find authentic Christianity, so Campbell declared, "All honour to those who have called us back to the real Jesus, the Jesus of Galilee and Jerusalem, the Jesus with the prophet's fire."[35] The New Theology rationalized Christianity through its application of contemporary biblical scholarship and scientific insights to urgent social and political questions. While explaining his reading of the atonement, the belief that sinful humanity was reconciled with God through the death of Jesus on the cross, R. J. Campbell emphasized the self-sacrifice of Jesus for the sake of others being the ultimate expression of God's loving being and God's will for the whole of creation. To illustrate his point and place it in the context of his day, Campbell declared, "Go with J. Keir Hardie to the House of Commons, and listen to his pleading for justice to his order, and you see the Atonement."[36] On July 31, 1907, Campbell announced

---

32. Campbell, *New Theology and Socialist*, 3.

33. Campbell, *New Theology*, 68.

34. Campbell, *New Theology*, 76.

35. Campbell, *New Theology*, 81.

36. Campbell, *New Theology*, 73.

his commitment to socialism as the practical, political expression of the teaching of Jesus.[37]

> To talk about the love of God would be rather meaning-less if the world had never known the love of Jesus. But now, the love, the very love that drove the Galilean Car-penter out into the open that He might tell about God to the toiling masses of His own day and generation, is up yonder in the heart of the Infinite, and up yonder is down here, in my heart too as well as yours.[38]

Time and again, throughout his national and international public life, Keir Hardie spoke of the importance of Jesus to his po-litical faith. From the platform of Labour Churches to the events shared with R. J. Campbell, and the Pentecost rally in Lille, the example of the self-giving service of the Carpenter from Nazareth who personified sacred solidarity was proclaimed. How Hardie viewed Jesus had been formed through the Morisonian Chris-tology of the Evangelical Union, Renan's life study, and the New Theology of Campbell's sermons, as well as his reflections upon the parallels between the suffering of the Galilean and the plight of workers in his time, including his own personal struggles. From suffering and plight came the realization that Jesus represented the ultimate truth that the bond between human beings was a sense of divinity, and, therefore, that was the basis of the politics that strove for justice and equality. Days before being part of the PSA delegation to Lille, Hardie had been one of the speakers at the 1910 Labour Week festival at Walworth's Browning Hall in London. His message was a familiar one to anyone who had heard Keir Har-die address an audience at any point during the previous twenty years because he spoke about the source of his inspiration and conviction.

> The impetus which drove me first of all into the Labour movement, and the inspiration which has carried me on to it, has been derived more from the teachings of

---

37. "Preacher Turns Socialist."
38. Campbell, *New Theology Sermons*, 56–57.

Jesus of Nazareth, than from all other sources combined. (Applause.) Labour men cannot afford, even if they were inclined, to neglect Christianity. A fact so potent in the history of the world, which has influenced not merely the life but the thought of a whole continent, which has its origins, by common consent, in the teachings and the life of a Common Working Man, must necessarily appeal to all who are seeking to-day to make life more worthy of its high purpose than it has been in the past.[39]

39. Ten Labour Members, *Labour and Religion*, 49.

2

The Kingdom of God

Towards the end of his life, he said that were he to live it again he would devote it to the advocacy of the Gospel of Christ. Perhaps this avowal was due to a sense of the failure of the Labour movement when faced by the crisis of the War, though he was conscious of the equal failure of the Church. Be that as it may, few men have done more to hasten the coming of the Kingdom of God on earth.[1]

IN 1907, ARCHIBALD FENNER BROCKWAY, who was writing for various newspapers by interviewing leading figures of the British Left such as H. G. Wells and George Bernard Shaw, arranged to speak to Keir Hardie on behalf of the *Daily News*. The outcome of that interview was the interviewer's conversion to the cause of socialism.[2] The son of British Christian missionaries in India, Fenner Brockway became a successor to Hardie as the editor of the *Labour Leader* in 1912. The quotation above comes from a chapter in a Student Christian Movement publication of 1927 entitled *Christian Social Reformers of the Nineteenth Century*, an interesting

1. Brockway, "James Keir Hardie," 239.
2. See Open University, "Fenner Brockway."

collection of short essays about Victorian activists including William Wilberforce, Florence Nightingale, Charles Dickens, William Morris, and James Keir Hardie. Fenner Brockway emphasizes the significance of Keir Hardie among the social reformers by drawing on the biblical subject of the kingdom of God, a theme that lies at the heart of Jesus' teaching as recorded in the Gospels of the New Testament.

Ernest Renan dedicated several chapters of his *Life of Jesus* to the kingdom of God, which he defines as "the reign of goodness."[3] According to his interpretation of Jesus' message, the kingdom of God will be established on earth once the evil that rules the world is conquered by the power of divine goodness.

> The advent of this reign of goodness will be a great and sudden revolution. The world will seem to be turned upside down; the actual state being bad, in order to represent the future, it suffices to conceive nearly the reverse of that which exists. The first shall be last. A new order shall govern humanity.[4]

The Jesus of Renan's study reaches a turning point in his life because of the realization that God was calling him to establish a new world order: "The persuasion that he was to establish the kingdom of God took absolute possession of his mind. He regarded himself as the universal reformer."[5] Describing the founder of Christianity as "the universal reformer" challenged how people perceived Jesus, because it is not a doctrinal statement but a term that resonated with social justice movements of the mid-nineteenth century. Interestingly, even though Renan claims that the fundamental idea of Jesus' teaching was a "radical revolution, embracing even nature itself,"[6] he goes on to state that Jesus rejected the revolutionary politics of groups, including the Zealots, that aimed to use force to drive out the occupying forces of Rome from Palestine.

3. Renan, *Life of Jesus*, 86.
4. Renan, *Life of Jesus*, 86.
5. Renan, *Life of Jesus*, 87.
6. Renan, *Life of Jesus*, 87.

For Renan, the revolution of the kingdom of God was moral and spiritual, changing the life of humanity and the whole of creation, not simply for one age but for all time to come. The moral and spiritual essence of society was developed in Renan's thinking about the nature of nationhood several decades later, when he said in a lecture, "A nation is a soul, a spiritual principle."[7] This talk of the moral and spiritual does not avoid addressing social injustice, because Renan's reading of Jesus' gospel is radical in its reordering of human relations.

> To whom should we turn, to whom should we trust to establish the kingdom of God? The mind of Jesus on this point never hesitated. That which is highly esteemed among men, is abomination in the sight of God. The founders of the kingdom of God are the simple. Not the rich, not the learned, not priests; but women, common people, the humble, and the young. The great characteristic of the Messiah is that "the poor have the gospel preached to them." [Matt. xi. 5.] The idyllic and gentle nature of Jesus here resumed the superiority. A great social revolution, in which rank will be overturned, in which all authority in this world will be humiliated, was his dream.[8]

In answer to the question "Do the churches heed the poor," Keir Hardie replied, "The 'Sermon on the Mount' is the panacea, not creeds. Doing, not believing, the former only makes one a Christian."[9] While the message that the kingdom of God was to be realized on earth is found throughout the teachings of Jesus in the Gospel accounts, the Sermon on the Mount is his longest continuous discourse on this core subject. Contained in chapters 5 to 7 of the Gospel of Matthew, and in a different form in chapter 6 of Luke's Gospel, this collection of sayings collated into one unified "sermon" includes the Beatitudes and the Lord's Prayer, which are the most widely known examples of Jesus' teaching on God's new

7. See Renan, "What Is a Nation?"
8. Renan, *Life of Jesus*, 92.
9. "Mr Keir Hardie and Congregationalists."

world, or kingdom on earth. According to Christian tradition, the Sermon on the Mount was delivered on a hill by the northwestern shore of the Sea of Galilee, the heartland of Jesus' ministry. In the Beatitudes, Jesus shines a light on those people regarded as unfortunate at best, but in reality, they were considered to be worthless by society, and he flips accepted moral values on their heads by declaring those very people to be at the top of the new social order in the kingdom of God on earth.

> When Jesus saw the crowds, he went up the mountain; and after he sat down, his disciples came to him. Then he began to speak, and taught them, saying:
>
> "Blessed are the poor in spirit, for theirs is the kingdom of heaven.
>
> Blessed are those who mourn, for they will be comforted.
>
> Blessed are the meek, for they will inherit the earth.
>
> Blessed are those who hunger and thirst for righteousness, for they will be filled.
>
> Blessed are the merciful, for they will receive mercy.
>
> Blessed are the pure in heart, for they will see God.
>
> Blessed are the peacemakers, for they will be called children of God.
>
> Blessed are those who are persecuted for righteousness sake, for theirs is the kingdom of heaven.
>
> Blessed are you when people revile you and persecute you and utter all kinds of evil against you falsely on my account. Rejoice and be glad, for your reward is great in heaven, for in the same way they persecuted the prophets who were before you." (Matt 5:1–12)

Luke's version of the Beatitudes found in the Sermon on the Plain[10] is distinctive from Matthew's in two ways: economic conditions

---

10. In this account Jesus had descended the mountain and preached to a crowd "on a level place" (Luke 6:17).

are addressed directly, and the blessings are followed by dire warnings for those who would find themselves last in the new order of the kingdom of God.

> Blessed are you who are poor, for yours is the kingdom of God.

> Blessed are you who are hungry now, for you will be filled. (Luke 6:20b–21a)

> But woe to you who are rich, for you have received your consolation.

> Woe to you who are full now, for you will be hungry. (Luke 6:24–25)

Often the Beatitudes of both Matthew and Luke are regarded together when reference is made to the Sermon on the Mount, which allows a roll call of the blessed as the poor, the hungry, the persecuted, the mournful, the merciful, the peacemakers, and those who strive for righteousness, while the rich and content are condemned. Renan, whose main Gospel source was John's account, draws on Matthew and Luke to speak of Jesus' discourse by the Sea of Galilee about the nature of God's kingdom: "The Sermon on the Mount, the apotheosis of the weak, the love of the people, regard for the poor, and the re-establishment of all that is humble, true, and simple."[11] In Keir Hardie's words, it was the putting into immediate action the ways of God's kingdom as defined by Jesus that mattered, not simply faith in "a hypothetical heaven in the future."[12]

Hardie often made the distinction between the Christianity of Jesus and the "Churchianity" of contemporary Christian denominations. His point was that the narrow religiosity of the Pharisees, condemned by Jesus because it stultified and diverted the earlier laws and prophetic teachings away from their sacred purposes, had been adopted by the Christian church. This was not only an attack on the life of the church for Keir Hardie, but it

---

11. Renan, *Life of Jesus*, 161.

12. "Mr Keir Hardie MP and Labour Church."

also had broader political implications. In an editorial for *Labour Leader* in 1900:

> Christ never once denounced the poor, weak erring sinner. He kept the invectives of His wrath for the clergy and the religious folk of His day. They, it was who blocked the way to the Kingdom. It is as true again as it was then, that for the meek, humble, contrite spirit of Jesus, we have to look to the outcast and fallen. The proud, bombastic, self-righteous spirit of Phariseeism dominates the Church and all its works. The modern Christian Church is a reflex of the modern business world, only more hateful because of the garb of unconscious hypocrisy in which it is arrayed.[13]

In 1901 the ILP published a tract entitled *Can a Man Be a Christian on a Pound a Week?*, which was Hardie's critique of current church theology and the "labour question" from his perspective of Jesus' teachings about the kingdom of God in the Sermon on the Mount. This was a scathing attack on what he considered to be the self-righteous hypocrisy of the institutional Christian denominations that justified economic, social, and political injustices because it was in their interests to do so. Under the section entitled "Kingdom of God," Hardie confronts his church-based targets:

> Christ laid down no elaborate system of either economics or theology. No great teacher ever did. His heart beat in sympathy with the great human heart of the race. His words are simple and not to be misunderstood when taken to mean what they say. His prayer—Thy Kingdom come, Thy will be done on earth as it is in Heaven—was surely meant to be taken literally. Are our opponents prepared to assert that in Heaven there will be factories working women and children for starvation wages; coal mines, and private property in land, dividing the population of Heaven into two classes, one revelling in riches and luxury, destructive of soul and body, the other grovelling in poverty, also destructive of all that is best in life? If not, how can they consistently support

13. Hardie, "Editorial" (1900).

the system which inevitably produces the state of things
upon earth?[14]

The response to this challenge, and by wider exposure to those
committed, or at least sympathetic, to the British labour movement from the ranks of the Christian churches, made Keir Hardie
modify his comments when he wrote what has been considered
to be the fullest exposition of his political thought, *From Serfdom
to Socialism*, published in 1907. Hardie writes, "The Sermon on
the Mount, whilst it perhaps lends but small countenance to State
Socialism, is full of the spirit of pure Communism."[15] Before the
term *communism* related to specific nations and governments
after the Russian Revolution of 1917, some democratic socialists
knowledgeable of the writings of Karl Marx and Friedrich Engels
incorporated the concept of communism into their thinking as a
vision of complete egalitarianism. This was the politics of human
solidarity that went beyond social and political reform to the total
transformation of the entire world order. William Morris's novel
News from Nowhere is a prime example of this interpretation (see
chapter 5), and Hardie followed suit, along with certain leading
figures from an array of denominations and traditions.

> It is not without significance that many of the best-
> known present-day leaders of religious thought are
> avowed Socialists in the modern sense of the word,
> and if they claim the right to call themselves Christian
> Socialists, no one who knows anything of the history of
> Christianity will challenge their right to use the prefix ...
> the Socialist who denounces rent and interest as robbery,
> and who seeks the abolition of the system which legal-
> izes such, is in the true line of apostolic succession with
> the pre-Christian era prophets, with the Divine Founder
> of Christianity, and with those who for the first seven
> hundred years of the Christian faith maintained even to
> the death and unsullied right of their religious faith to be
> regarded as the Gospel of the poor. Surely if Socialism
> can enable man

14. Hardie, *Can a Man*, 17.
15. Hardie, *From Serfdom*, 83.

To stand from fear set free, to breathe and wait.
To hold a hand uplifted over Hate,
it will be, if not religion in itself, at least a handmaiden to religion, and as such entitled to the support of all who pray for the
coming of Christ's Kingdom upon earth.[16]

One of "the best-known present-day leaders of religious
thought [who] are avowed Socialists in the modern sense of the
word" was R. J. Campbell.[17] On March 25, 1907, Campbell shared
a platform at a Liverpool ILP meeting with national leaders of
the British labour movement, including Bruce Glasier, Ramsay
MacDonald, and Keir Hardie. His lecture at that event was published the following year as a booklet entitled *The New Theology
and the Socialist Movement*. From the outset, Campbell claims that
the New Theology that he proclaimed from the pulpit of the City
Temple is the theological basis of the labour movement because
it is "the theology of the Kingdom of God."[18] He proceeds by giving a potted history of the Jewish people, stating that by the time
Jesus was born, they were "an oppressed people, a suffering people,
a poverty-stricken people; they were ground under the heel of a
worldwide empire, the empire of Rome."[19] At that moment of their
story, the Jewish people began to hark back to what they considered to be the golden era of King David's reign a thousand years
earlier, and they dreamt of a son of David, or messiah, who would
instigate a new chapter for their nation with the defeat of the occupying forces of Rome and reestablishment of sacred laws—in
other words, the kingdom of God on earth.

> Then Jesus Came, and He gathered them around Him
> on the hillsides of Galilee, and this is the way He talked,
> "Don't you imagine that the Kingdom of God is coming
> like a thunder-clap, because it is not. Don't you think that
> simply because you are descended from Abraham you
> are going to be favourites of Heaven—because you are

16. Hardie, *From Serfdom*, 87–88.
17. Hardie, *From Serfdom*, 87.
18. Campbell, *New Theology and Socialist*, 8.
19. Campbell, *New Theology and Socialist*, 10.

not. The Kingdom of God is a kingdom of love—a kingdom of universal brotherhood, a kingdom where every
man deals justly with his neighbour. It simply means the
reign of God in the hearts of men." (Cheers.) Then He
went on to say, "Begin here and now to expect it, and
work for it, and pray for it, 'Thy will be done on earth as
it is done in Heaven. Thy kingdom come.'" "Say not, Lo
here, neither, Lo there. Behold, the kingdom of God is
within you."[20]

Campbell continues in the lecture by saying that the reason for
Jesus' execution on the cross was that Jesus refused to use violence
to bring about the kingdom of God because that would have been
to contradict his teaching, which reflected the peaceful nature of
God's will. After his death, those ordinary, working people whose
lives had been transformed by encountering him and his message
formed a society or ecclesia in the name of Jesus. Then, tying together that fledgling Christian movement of the mid-first century
with the labour movement in the early twentieth century, R. J.
Campbell makes a bold statement, which receives great acclama-
tion from his Liverpool audience:

> The "Ecclesia" of Jesus was the beginning of the Church
> of Jesus, as it has now come to be called. "Church" means
> society, assembly, organisation, and that society, assem-
> bly, organisation of the first Christian century was what
> the Labour Party is now—(hear, hear)—the organisa-
> tion that meant to try to realise the Kingdom of God.
> (Cheers)[21]

This belief that the labour movement was the vehicle by which
God's new world was to be established is echoed in Keir Hardie's
speeches and writings. In an exposition of the ILP's ethical and
theological principles, Hardie writes that a committed member "is
at bottom a religious enthusiast lured on by his vision of a Kingdom of God upon Earth. Nothing else explains the enthusiasm of

---

20. Campbell, *New Theology and Socialist*, 10–11.
21. Campbell, *New Theology and Socialist*, 12.

the Independent Labour Party."[22] Also, he felt that working people had discovered the same truth, that their efforts to secure a more just society were better placed in gathering people dedicated to realizing greater human solidarity through political change, than in Christian denominations that were more concerned with the preservation of their institutions. The goal of the kingdom of God was universal kinship, and the means of achieving it was the politics of the labour movement.

> If Labour men had left the churches, it was because they believed them to be unsympathetic to their ideals and emphasised a spirituality which spoke of the kingdom of God as a heaven that was to be in the world beyond and not as Christ meant—establishment here upon earth.[23]

Consistently throughout his political life, Hardie's call to both the Christian churches and the labour movement was for them to claim their true purpose, to be the heralds of a complete reordering of human relationships as envisaged by Jesus of Nazareth. For the churches, this was a return to their origins, and for his contemporary Labour comrades, it was a theological rephrasing of their cause. Such a reassessment by both socialists and Christians would lead them to discover that they were natural allies because their aims and values were shared.

Rooted in the gospel of Jesus as proclaimed in the Sermon on the Mount, Keir Hardie's socialism was what he regarded as the political manifesto for the kingdom of God on earth. A new world order through the "reign of goodness," as Renan defined it, was good news to the ears of the poor, the hungry, the peacemakers, and those who strive for righteousness, but not so to the rich, content, complacent, and those who seek the preservation of the status quo. The statement made by R. J. Campbell that what underpinned the labour movement was the theology of the kingdom of God sums up Keir Hardie's foundational conviction and constant motivation for his faith in politics. The new world order of universal

22. Hardie, *ILP*, 6.
23. "Mr Keir Hardie's Confession."

kinship as empowered by socialism was pivotal. Hardie used the language of God's kingdom unashamedly to describe his vision for British society and the wider world, because for him "Christ's teaching should appeal with irresistible power"[24] to socialists, Labour activists, and anyone who was committed to the cause of human solidarity.

24. Ten Labour Members, *Labour and Religion*, 51.

3

Prophecy & Practice

On Sunday 27 March, at Mansfield House university settlement, Canning Town, he [Keir Hardie] preached an afternoon sermon on the prophet Elijah and God's "still small voice" (1 Kings, 19.11), and in the evening adopted a prophetic role himself, with a lecture urging the formation of an independent labour party.[1]

THIS NEWSPAPER CLIPPING FROM 1892 encapsulates in one sentence (above) the importance of the prophetic tradition to Keir Hardie's creed and public persona. He drew on the teachings of the Old Testament prophets and, in turn, was a prophetic figure for his day. The setting of Hardie's sermon and lecture on that Sunday in March was Mansfield House, part of the settlement movement, which sought social reform by establishing communal-based houses in poor, urban communities, offering education, healthcare, and leisure activities. Many of the settlement houses were sponsored by universities and colleges, with their students dedicating time to live and work in them. Mansfield House was founded in 1890 in the Canning Town area of West Ham, East London by the Congregationalist ministerial training institution

1. "Mr Keir Hardie at Mansfield House."

Mansfield College in Oxford.[2] Hardie took the opportunity at Mansfield House of speaking to a gathering of people who were committed to social justice through local action by recalling Elijah, a prophet commissioned by God to overcome injustice and restore the people of Israel to their sacred roots. Later that day, according to the newspaper article, Hardie claimed Elijah's mantle, like his disciple Elisha, by arguing for the liberation of working-class politics.

Prophecy and the prophetic tradition lie at the heart of Jewish Scriptures. The teachings of the prophets were recorded, reflected upon, and reinterpreted by generations, through periods of war, occupation, and exile, as well as in times of peace, stability, and prosperity. The Hebrew origins of the word *prophet* offer an insight into the role and practice of these historical figures for the theology and identity of Judaism. In the earlier Scriptures the prophet is referred to as a "seer" (1 Sam 9:9) or a "discerner" (2 Sam 24:11; Amos 7:12), which emphasizes the mystical nature of foreseeing the consequences of diverting from or completely disowning the will of God. Divine will was expressed in the laws of the Torah or Pentateuch (the five books of Moses: Genesis, Exodus, Leviticus, Numbers, and Deuteronomy). The term *prophet* was often used to mean someone called or commissioned, "the official standing of the one who carries the title as a spokesperson chosen by God to deliver a message in God's name."[3] There are various examples in Jewish Scripture of prophets delivering their divine message through symbolic acts as warnings to their contemporaries and descendants. Jeremiah smashes a clay jar as a sign of the fragility of the nation (Jer 19:10), and Isaiah walks naked and barefooted for three years to signify the forthcoming captivity in Assyria (Isa 20:3). These were powerful parables enacted for dramatic and lasting effect. But the designation of Hebrew Scriptures as the Old Testament in the Christian biblical canon has reduced the Jewish prophets to foretellers of the "Christ-event," thus diminishing the importance of their status and the potency of their message for

2. Inglis, *Churches and Working Classes*, 159.

3. Ceresko, *Introduction to Old Testament*, 166.

Jewish faith and history. Although appreciated and honored with hindsight, the Hebrew prophets were castigated in their times, one example being Elijah, the prophet referred to in Keir Hardie's sermon at Mansfield House, a prophet who was called the "troubler of Israel" by Israel's king, Ahab (1 Kgs 18:17).

When Keir Hardie pointed to the Jewish prophets, he did so to acknowledge them as a movement for social liberation, and not merely as the precursors to Christianity. One of the chapters of *From Serfdom to Socialism* delves into the theological sources of Hardie's political cause, and Hardie thanks Ernest Renan for making him realize the relevance of the Jewish prophetic tradition for the cause of social liberation in his age:

> The prophets of Israel are fiery publicists of the description we should now call Socialists or Anarchists. They are fanatical in their demands for social justice and proclaim aloud that, if the world is not just nor capable of becoming just, it were better it were destroyed.[4]

Hardie embraced contemporaries he considered to be within the prophetic tradition who were often excluded from the global community of the labour movement. One example is the expulsion of anarchists from the Second International Congress in London of 1896 over the issue of commitment to parliamentary democracy. This exclusion occurred even though the anarchist leaders, including Domela Nieuwenhuis and Louise Michel, had been welcomed by the British hosts and spoke at the public rally in Trafalgar Square.[5] So, to include those whose ideology rejected state government for nonhierarchical, self-sufficient, interdependent communities is an indication of Hardie's openness to the politics of people who didn't share his lifelong crusade to reform the democratic structures and processes of British society. The implication of the previous quotation from Hardie's *From Serfdom to Socialism* is a willingness to accept the radical challenge of the prophetic tradition, which demanded social justice and offered a vision of godly

4. Hardie, *From Serfdom*, 82–83.
5. Wrigley, "ILP and Second International," 301.

egalitarianism for humanity and the whole of creation. Keir Hardie sought allies for the sake of the sacred cause of universal solidarity and was willing to believe that the movement was both broad and deep in terms of political philosophies and historical roots.

In an appraisal of Karl Marx published in 1911, Keir Hardie reflects on the revolutionary nature of socialism by looking to a figure considered to be a bridge between the Old and New Testaments of Christian Scripture, John the Baptist: "But is not, it may be asked, Socialism a revolutionary movement? Yes, no such revolutionary change has been conceived since the days 2,000 years ago, when John the Baptist called upon men to repent for the Kingdom of God was at hand!"[6] Hardie develops his argument by relating John the Baptist, who prepared the way and heralded the ministry of Jesus of Nazareth and his gospel of the kingdom of God, to Marx, whose writings he considered to be preparing the way and heralding the classless, socialist state—the political manifestation of God's kingdom on earth (this will be explored further in a later chapter).

Revered as a prophet in Christianity, Islam, the Bahá'í Faith, and most notably in Mandaeism, John the Baptist, or Baptizer, was an itinerant preacher of the first century CE, who conducted his ministry in the wilderness, the desert area of Judea that lies to the east of Jerusalem, descending to the Dead Sea. According to all four of the New Testament Gospel writers, John's message was one of repentance, a call for people to turn their lives around and live by the values declared by the prophets who had preceded him. The symbolic act of repentance was baptism, and for those who were attracted to John this meant immersion in the River Jordan, the river that the people of Israel had crossed to reach the land promised to them through the prophecies of their leader Moses. Mark's Gospel account, which is widely regarded as the earliest of the Gospels, links the ministry of John the Baptist to earlier prophecies from Jewish history:

As it is written in the prophet Isaiah,

---

6. Hardie, *Karl Marx*, 15.

"See, I am sending my messenger ahead of you,
who will prepare your way;
the voice of one crying out in the wilderness:
'Prepare the way of the Lord,
make his paths straight,'"
John the Baptizer appeared in the wilderness, proclaiming a
baptism of repentance for the forgiveness of sins. (Mark 1:2–4,
referencing Mal 3:1 and Isa 40:3)

Alongside references in the New Testament, the first-century
Romano-Jewish historian Flavius Josephus recorded the role that
John played in his sociopolitical context. Josephus was born in
Jerusalem around 37 CE and died sixty-three years later in Rome
as a citizen of its empire, so it may not be surprising to note that
his account of events in Palestine in the years preceding his birth
was pro-Roman. It is with that understanding of this bias to the
dominant force of his time and place that we read Josephus's account of John the Baptist's fate at the hands of Herod Antipas, the
puppet-ruler of Galilee.

Some Jews thought that the destruction of Herod's army
came from God, and very justly so, as punishment for his
treatment of John, who was called the Baptist. For Herod
[Antipas] had John executed, though he was a good man
and commanded the Jews to exercise virtue through justice towards one another and piety towards God and by
doing so to arrive at immersion, for immersion would be
acceptable to God only if practiced not to expiate sins but
for purification of the body after the soul had first been
thoroughly purified by righteousness.
Because, affected by his words, many flocked to him,
Herod feared that John's great influence over the people
might lead to revolt (for the people seemed likely to do
whatever he counselled).[7]

Keir Hardie's take on John the Baptist as a revolutionary
leader is certainly in line with Josephus, whose *Antiquities of the
Jews* was an important primary source for Ernest Renan's *Life of
Jesus*. Renan writes of John, "Like the ancient Jewish prophets, he

7. Josephus, *Antiquities*, 146.

was, in the highest degree, a censor of the established powers."[8] In a scathing attack on the Christian churches, Hardie calls upon the revolutionary spirit of John the Baptist and Jesus of Nazareth to purge and purify what he describes as genteel assemblies that act as if they were the faithful disciples of Herod Antipas:

> The burning sarcasms of John the Baptist and Jesus would s soon cleanse the Churches, which are now noth-ing but "whitewashed graves." To-day there are sufficient Churches in the land to be-head a hundred a John the Baptist and crucify a thousand Saviours.[9]

It was not enough to take heed of the prophets; for Hardie there was a need for repentance leading to action so that their vision of a godly egalitarianism could become a reality. This turning life around to the ways that the prophets recalled was as much a plea to the labour movement as to the Christian church. So, it was to the earliest times of the first followers of Jesus that Keir Hardie pointed out as a model of a sacred socialist society in practice. In the previous chapter about the importance of the kingdom of God to Hardie's creed, we touched on how Hardie and others like R. J. Campbell referred to the early church as an example to both Labour and church, alike. The key biblical passages offering an insight into the primary Christian community in Jerusalem are found in the first chapters of the Acts of the Apostles in the New Testament. Acts claims to share the same author of Luke's Gos-pel, and so together the two books are an account of the life and ministry of Jesus of Nazareth and the story of his followers in the succeeding decades as they revealed his message across the Roman Empire. The passages in Acts of particular interest are accounts of the first Christian congregation in the days following the Jewish harvest festival of Shavuot or Pentecost, which for them meant a spirit-filled empowerment.

> All who believed were together and had all things in common; they would sell their possessions and goods

8. Renan, *Life of Jesus*, 83.
9. "Mr Keir Hardie and Congregationalists."

and distribute the proceeds to all, as any had need. (Acts 2:44–45)

Now the whole group of those who believed were of one heart and soul, and no one claimed private ownership of any possessions, but everything they owned was held in common. (Acts 4:32)

There was not a needy person among them, for as many as owned lands or houses sold them and brought the proceeds of what was sold. They laid it at the apostles' feet, and it was distributed to each as any had need. (Acts 4:34–35)

The original expression of Christianity has been described as Christian communism, with all distinctions between its members eradicated by the universality of the congregation's egalitarian communal life. Mexican biblical scholar and philosopher José Porfirio Miranda commentates on the key passages from Acts by noticing that during those post-Pentecost days in Jerusalem if people wanted to belong to the fledgling community of Jesus "the condition was communism."[10]

Keir Hardie gives his commentary on the key verses from Acts 4 in his tract *Can a Man Be a Christian on a Pound a Week?*, first published in 1901:

Here we have it clearly brought out that the direct outcome of the teachings of Jesus upon those who lived nearest to His time, and who became His followers, was to make them Communists. These early Christians found it impossible to retain possession of private property after they became Christians, since it raised artificial class distinctions in their midst and prevented the free play of that spirit of fraternal brotherhood which Jesus taught as one of the characteristics of the Kingdom of God. And if that was so in the earlier days of Christianity, it would be equally true of its later years if Christianity were still being preached and practised.[11]

10. Miranda, *Communism in the Bible*, 7.
11. Hardie, *Can a Man*, 11.

Five years previously Hardie had attended a performance of the melodrama *The Sign of the Cross* by the English actor and playwright Wilson Barrett. The play told a story set in Rome during the reign of Nero in the mid-first century CE, when the followers of Jesus were being vigorously and viciously persecuted. The main character is Marcus Superbus, a member of a ruling-class patrician family, who falls in love with a young woman, Mercia, and converts to Christianity because of her; this leads to the dramatic climax of the play, when both are sacrificed to the lions in the arena. Moved by the play, Keir Hardie shared his reflections on the courageous faith of the first generation of Christians compared to the comfortable complacency of those purporting to follow Jesus Christ at the end of the nineteenth century.

> I watched closely the parsons who sat near me whilst the play proceeded, and of all the spectators in the theatre, they seemed the least moved by the tragedy which the persecution of the early Christians represented. On the stage were the men who won the world for Christ—poor men, haggard, ill-fed, impetuous, enthusiastic, trudging from village to village and city to city, carrying the "glad tidings"—shut up in prisons, murdered in the streets, torn to pieces by wild beasts, dipped in tar and set alight, to enable the gladiators to see the trembling, non-resisting victims whom they were to torture and put to death. These were the "Christian ministers" of the beginning. Those of to-day, close-shaven, well-fed, sleek, aesthetic, dressed in broadcloth, unemotional, and thanking God that their lines had been cast in more pleasant places. Does not the contrast painfully reveal what is going on in our midst? Christianity is no longer a reality. The religious form may still exist, but once again the spirit has passed away and has found its embodiment elsewhere. The unthinking mob then, as now, were ready at the bidding of Nero the tyrant, to stone and betray the reformers, and believe all manner of evil of them. And the priests of that day were on the side of Nero, as they mostly are to-day. The times have changed; so, too, has the scene of action, but the central facts remain the

same. Only through tears and sacrifice has progress been possible in the past, and just as the reformers of to-day are prepared to give up everything for the cause, so shall the measure of our progress be. Have we learned the lesson?[12]

Twenty years to the month after he addressed the Mansfield House university settlement with prophetic spirit, Hardie spoke about early Christian communism in a lecture on March 3, 1912, to the Adult School Union at Dowlais in his parliamentary constituency of Merthyr Tydfil in the South Wales Valleys. He had reached the same conclusion as José Porfirio Miranda would many decades later, that "the very fact of becoming a Christian carried with it the obligation to be at the same time a Communist in all that pertained to the things of life."[13] Such was the draw of the alternative way of Christian living that it attracted mainly slaves and poor workers, leading to the suspicion of the rich and ruling classes, who regarded Christian congregations as rebel cells that threatened the welfare of the Roman Empire. The rot set into the church when Christianity was adopted as the official religion of the empire after 312 CE, in Hardie's words, "from the time that Constantine began to pay lip service to the doctrines of Jesus."[14] The example of the conversion of the Roman emperor symbolized for Keir Hardie the repeated fate of radical religion, as soon as it was approved of, then authorized by those with power in society. It betrayed its roots, and at that point in time the prophetic tradition was relevant once again in recalling and retelling its powerful message to the world. Hardie's political life meant adopting the prophetic role for his day, taking on the mantle of Elijah, Isaiah, and John the Baptist as he revived their movement by being a "troubler of the nation" with a vision of an alternative world. Hardie reminded the people of the sacred cause of justice, peace, and human solidarity, and pointed them to God's kingdom or new world that could be manifested as godly egalitarianism in a future socialist state, the like of which

12. Hardie, "Comments."
13. "Mr Keir Hardie MP at Dowlais."
14. "Mr Keir Hardie MP at Dowlais."

had been realized among the earliest Christians. His imagery and phraseology were no mere rhetorical tropes to stir the crowds for their votes. The prophetic announcements of Keir Hardie were underpinned by the knowledge and commitment that the transformation of society begins with improving the lives of its people who are the most marginalized and powerless.

> Socialists, in common with the early Christian fathers, recognise that it is futile to proclaim fraternity and community of interest unless they at the same time provide the environment and conditions of life which make these possible.[15]

15. Hardie, *From Serfdom*, 86.

4

Religion of Humanity

Hardie's Socialism can neither be classified as scientific or Utopian. . . . So far as he was influenced towards Socialism by the ideas of others, it was as he himself stated, by the Bible, the songs of Burns, the writings of Carlyle, Ruskin and Mill, and the democratic tradition in the working-class homes in Scotland in his early days. In the main, however, as with many of us, he derived his Socialism from his own thought and feeling, the plight of the workers, and the state of the world. He was guided by religious, or perhaps I should say, moral convictions, rather than by philosophical theorising or scientific analyses of economic or social phenomena.[1]

A S THESE WORDS OF his comrade John Bruce Glasier indicate, Keir Hardie's thinking was shaped by a wide range of sources. This chapter is an exploration of the breadth of his influences. From an early appreciation of Robert Burns's poetry, Hardie became aware of some of the most significant thinkers of the nineteenth century in Britain and the United States, including

1. Glasier, *Keir Hardie*, 10.

philosophers and social commentators, such as Thomas Carlyle, John Stuart Mill, John Ruskin, and Ralph Waldo Emerson, and the poet Walt Whitman. He gained inspiration from his reading of radical history, which offered an alternative to the authorized version about those wielding power because it told the story of the people of Britain and Europe and their struggle for justice, freedom, and solidarity across the centuries. Then there was Hardie's growing openness to the insights of different faith traditions and spiritualities, including Buddhism, Islam, and the Bahá'í Faith. Keir Hardie sought truth in what he read, in the places he visited, and in the people he encountered, so that when he gained a new understanding, he weaved its perception into his moral convictions and creed, forming a religion of humanity.

"I owe more to Robert Burns than to any other man alive or dead," Keir Hardie wrote in *Labour Leader* in 1909, "I had imbibed the liberty-loving spirit and humanitarianism of Burns."[2] The Scottish poet and lyricist, Robert Burns, is commonly celebrated as the national poet of Scotland, and he has received international recognition for his work. The "Ploughman Poet" was an early exponent of what became the Romantic movement, a cultural force from the late eighteenth and through the nineteenth centuries, which praised the natural world and the glories of the past, emphasizing emotional and individual impulses. Burns's poetry shows shrewd discernment of the human spirit and often expresses his radical egalitarian views. After he died in 1796 at the age of thirty-seven years, Robert Burns became a symbol of Scottish identity to his home nation and among members of the scattered, international Scottish diaspora. Throughout the following century, his image and poetry were championed by radical liberals and socialists because of his empathy with the poor and oppressed, and his expressions of support for revolutionary causes. In one late poem, "A Man's a Man for A' That," Burns's egalitarian call for human solidarity is clearly stated. The final verse reads,

Then let us pray that come it may—

2. Hardie, "Editorial" (1909).

As come it will for a' that—
That sense and worth, o'er a' the earth,
Shall bear the gree, an' a' that.
For a' that, an' a' that,
It's coming yet for a' that,
That man to man, the world o'er,
Shall brothers be for a' that.[3]

By the time Keir Hardie was born, Robert Burns had become a cultural icon, with the nobler aspects of his work, personality, and image promoted and elevated.[4] Along with J. Bruce Glasier, Hardie's biographers have commented on the inspiration Hardie received from Burns. According to John C. Kenworthy, the founder of the Brotherhood Church, in an article of 1894, "Robert Burns sang democracy into him."[5] Eighty years later Iain McLean would write in his account of Hardie's life:

> A creed of socialism based on Robert Burns was not only, in Hardie's view, more humane than one based on Karl Marx, it was also more likely to gain working-class support. . . . And it is Hardie's vision of socialism which has been shared by most members of the Labour Party throughout its lifetime.[6]

Keir Hardie regarded Robert Burns as "an articulate peasant" for whom some "common-place incident of everyday occurrence touched his sympathy, and from that he deduced a moral of general application."[7] On Burns's affinity with working people, Hardie writes, "He was essentially one of themselves—human in every fibre of his being, every nerve tingling with sympathy for sorrow and suffering wherever found."[8] What the two men shared in their attitude to life and its struggles was a raw, romantic radicalism, envisaging universal solidarity or kinship through everyday encounters.

3. R. Burns, *Complete Poems and Songs*, 415–16.

4. Wilson, *Inside the Mind*.

5. Kenworthy, "J. Keir Hardie, M.P."

6. McLean, *Keir Hardie*, 172.

7. Hardie, "Editorial" (1909).

8. Hardie, "Editorial" (1909).

Hardie once described himself "as a man who worshipped at the shrine of Robert Burns as he worshipped at the shrine of no other human being,"[9] the Ploughman Poet being but one step removed from the divine humanity found in Jesus of Nazareth.

Another shrine that Keir Hardie claimed to be the focus of his adoration was that of Thomas Carlyle's. A fellow lowland Scot like Burns, Carlyle was a highly influential polymath who excelled in history, philosophy, mathematics, translation, literary criticism, and satirical writing. One main concern through his extensive work was that the nature, demands, and consequences of the rapidly growing industrial society needed to be carefully studied and analyzed, which resonated with the mood and fear of early Victorian Britain of the 1830s and 1840s. But as social attitudes became more relaxed to the outcomes of industrialization from the middle of the century onwards, Carlyle became more strident in the tone of his statements, leading to accusations in the twentieth century of racism and that he was "one of the intellectual founding fathers of fascism."[10] Hardie's attitude to Thomas Carlyle changes over the years. In 1894 Hardie was calling him one of "the Pioneers of the Independent Labour Party" alongside John Ruskin, calling them "the prophets of this generation . . . just as Isaiah and Jeremiah and all the rest of them were the prophets their days."[11] According to John C. Kenworthy, Carlyle had "cast his spell upon him."[12] But by 1909 Hardie wrote that he had learned about Carlyle's failings and weaknesses, so he was something of a past hero; yet Hardie continued to cite his earliest major work as a major influence: "I mark the reading of 'Sartor,' however, as a real turning point, and went through the book three times in succession until the spirit of it somewhat entered into me."[13]

Sartor Resartus, which can be translated as "The Tailor Re-tailored," was first published in installments in *Fraser's Magazine*

9. "Mr Keir Hardie MP in Cheltenham."

10. Keating, *Victorian Prophets*, 44.

11. "Mr Hardie MP in Manchester."

12. Kenworthy, "J. Keir Hardie, M.P."

13. Hughes, *Keir Hardie's Speeches*, 138.

between 1833 and 1834. The work claims to be the musings of a German philosopher of clothes called Diogenes Teufelsdröckh, who was a figment of Carlyle's imagination. Through satire, Carlyle can take the reader on an existential journey of discovery as Teufelsdröckh wrestles with the issues of contemporary society, attacking utilitarianism and commercialization along the way, yet remaining faithful to the potential of the human spirit.

> It is, that Teufelsdröckh is not without some touch of the universal feeling, a wish to proselytise. . . . Remarkable, moreover is this saying of his: ". . . A man, be the Heavens ever praised, is sufficient for himself; yet were ten men, united in Love, capable of being and of doing what ten thousand singly would fail in. Infinite is the help man can yield to man." And now in conjunction therewith consider this other: "It is the Night of the World, and still long till it be Day; we wander amid the glimmer of smoking ruins, and the Sun and the Stars of Heaven are as if blotted out for a season."[14]

Thomas Carlyle's work raised questions about the state of society in Keir Hardie's mind, questions that gave him an insight into the causes of suffering and exploitation, which would lead him to socialism as the only means of realizing true justice.[15] *Sartor Resartus* set Hardie on the path to socialism, because for him, to echo Carlyle's words, it alone could unite humanity in love during "the Night of the World."

Referring to Hardie's speech about the pioneers of the ILP delivered to a Labour Church gathering in Saint James' Hall, Manchester, in January 1894, the "Jeremiah" to Thomas Carlyle's "Isaiah" was John Ruskin. Art critic, philosopher, and social commentator, Ruskin was a prophet of the Victorian age. In contrast to Thomas Carlyle, the reputation of John Ruskin's public contribution has been reappraised and acknowledged as a proto-environmentalism, with a commitment to sustainability and the significance of the crafts. Ruskin came to prominence with the first

14. Carlyle, *Sartor Resartus*, 180.
15. Hughes, *Keir Hardie's Speeches*, 138.

volume of *Modern Painters* in 1843, in which he defended rigorously the work of J. M. W. Turner, arguing that his art was true to the natural world, which Ruskin stated was the prime calling of an artist. In the following decade, Ruskin championed the work and philosophy of the Pre-Raphaelite artists, who had been influenced by his beliefs. His extended essay "Unto This Last," first published between 1860 and 1862, indicated growing concern about social and political issues. The title of the work comes from Jesus' parable of the workers in the vineyard:

> I will give unto this last, even as unto thee. Is it not lawful for me to do what I will with mine own? Is thine eye evil, because I am good? So the last shall be first, and the first last: for many be called, but few chosen. (Matt 20:14–16 KJV)

In the parable, all the workers are paid equally, no matter how many hours they worked. Ruskin offered an interpretation based on social and economic implications, which included the introduction of a living wage.

> There is no wealth but life. Life, including all its powers of love, of joy, and of admiration. That country is the richest which nourishes the greatest number of noble and happy human beings; that man is richest who, having perfected the functions of his own life to the utmost, has always the widest helpful influence, both personal, and by means of his possessions, over the lives of others.[16]

From 1871, John Ruskin started writing open letters to the workers of Britain, which were published until 1884 as monthly tracts with the title *Fors Clavigera*. What developed through these writings were concepts, principles, and programs that formed the basis of Ruskin's visionary nation, a cooperative, cultured society where arts and crafts were treasured as artistic professions. Ten years after the final tract, Keir Hardie in Saint James' Hall spoke of its author's prophetic warning to the actual society of the day:

16. Ruskin, "Unto This Last," 105.

> The message which John Ruskin gave to the people of
> this generation was that wealth was only valuable in
> so far as it tended to promote human happiness—that
> wealth, while it might be blessing might curse—and he
> warned the nation against believing it had got hold of
> wealth while in reality wealth had got hold of it.[17]

Contemporary to Carlyle and Ruskin, John Stuart Mill was
one of the most influential thinkers of the era. Mill was home-
schooled by his father, the historian James Mill, a dedicated disciple of utilitarian philosopher Jeremy Bentham, who defined the
"fundamental axiom" of his philosophy to be the principle that "it
is the greatest happiness of the greatest number that is the measure of right and wrong."[18] J. S. Mill's educational background was
intended to instill the value of utilitarianism as an ethical theory,
economic agenda, and political philosophy, just as much as a
faith-based school would have grounded its curriculum in the authorized doctrines and moral teachings of its sponsoring denomination or tradition. His father's approach to intellectual formation
was highly successful, as J. S. Mill became a leading exponent of
utilitarianism through his parallel careers as a social philosopher,
political economist, and Liberal politician. Such was his concern
for the freedom of humanity that Mill reacted against any dog-
matic ideology, including narrow interpretations of utilitarian
theories.[19] His most enduring work was published in 1859 under
the title *On Liberty*, in which Mill discusses civil or social liberty,
which he defines as "the nature and limits of the power which can
be legitimately exercised by society over the individual."[20] Building
upon the thoughts of his predecessor Bentham, Mill hones in on
the fundamental objective of the philosophy:

> I regard utility as the ultimate appeal on all ethical
> questions; but it must be utility in the largest sense,

17. "Mr Hardie MP in Manchester."
18. J. Burns and Hart, *Comment on the Commentaries*, 393.
19. Keating, *Victorian Prophets*, 69.
20. Mill, *On Liberty*, 1.

grounded on the permanent interests of man as a progressive being.[21]

The thrust of the argument of *On Liberty* is that individual freedom must take precedence over uncontrolled social control by
the nation-state. Keir Hardie's references to J. S. Mill placed him
within the context of the evolutionary thinking of the early to
mid-nineteenth century, which paved the way for the democratic
socialism of the later decades by holding together personal liberty
in terms of a just society.[22] What drew Hardie and Mill together as
public figures, though from different generations, was their cham-
pioning of women's suffrage. Mill wrote *The Subjection of Women*,
published in 1869, regarded as an early defense of feminism, and
he was the second MP, after the Chartist Henry Hunt, to argue for
the democratic rights of women. Hardie claimed the Liberal J. S.
Mill for the labour cause, declaring the posthumous conversion of
the utilitarian philosopher to socialism in one of his parliamentary
speeches.[23]

Keir Hardie was weaving a colorful tapestry from the
threads of his reading of the Judeo-Christian tradition, the radical Romanticism of Burns's poetry, and the social philosophies
of the Victorian prophets, as he developed his understanding of
the religion of humanity. Two other contemporary figures whom
Hardie honored for their influence on his worldview were tower-
ing figures of American thought, Ralph Waldo Emerson and Walt
Whitman. In an article from 1909 published in *Labour Leader*,
Hardie recognized both men as successors to Robert Burns in
terms of his own intellectual growth.[24] Emerson, an essayist, poet,
and philosopher, was the "leading light" of the Transcendentalist
movement. Relating the Unitarian theology of the oneness of God
to an appreciation of different religious traditions, especially Hin-
duism, led to a conception of the "Over Soul"; and the emphasis

21. Mill, *On Liberty*, 15.
22. "Keir Hardie on Continent."
23. Hughes, *Keir Hardie's Speeches*, 107.
24. Hardie, "Editorial" (1909).

of Romanticism on human potential, Transcendentalism, under Emerson's guidance, stressed the importance of self-reliance, self-culture, and individual expression. Such emphases were placed over and against the demands on the individual by the growing governmental apparatus of the United States. Emerson's renowned essay of 1841, "Self-Reliance," begins with a Latin quotation that can be translated into English as "Do not seek things outside of yourself."[25] Emerson expands upon the phrase:

> This is the ultimate fact which we so quickly reach on this [self-reliance] as on every topic, the resolution of all into the ever-blessed *one*. Self-existence is the attribute of the Supreme cause.[26]

This essay is attributed to be the spark that ignited the Transcendentalist spirit, inspiring many of Emerson's fellow citizens to re-define their national identity at a time when new settlements and communities were being formed across the country.

> It is easy to see that a greater self-reliance must work a revolution in all the offices and relations of men; in their religion; in their education; in their pursuits; their moods of living; their association; in their property; in their respective views.[27]

Throughout the essay, Emerson repeats a call that would have resounded with Keir Hardie as it stirred his heart: "Whoso would be a man must be a nonconformist."[28]

In the same vein, but more liberated in spirit, Walt Whitman personified the Transcendentalist ideal of the free individual. His poetry celebrates the dynamic nature of humanity; though life is lived personally, it is so through the bonds of our common being. It has been commented that Whitman's work marks a transition from the Transcendentalist belief in the "Over Soul" to the realist position of avoiding or redefining the supernatural. This bridging

25. Emerson, *Self-Reliance*, 19.
26. Emerson, *Self-Reliance*, 30 (emphasis original).
27. Emerson, *Self-Reliance*, 32–33.
28. Emerson, *Self-Reliance*, 21.

of the sacred realm towards the gritty, everyday existence of Whitman's city neighbors is reflected in a remark by Emerson about Whitman's epic collection of poems *Leaves of Grass*, that it was a "combination of the *Bhagavad-Gita* and the *New York Herald*."[29] Walt Whitman published the first edition of *Leaves of Grass* in 1855, and he continued to revise and expand on the poems until he died in 1892. The purpose of his life's work was to connect with working-class Americans and offer them insights and a language for them to interpret their lives individually and communally, as Emerson had for his intellectual peers.

> One's-Self I sing, a simple separate person,
> Yet utter the word Democratic, the word En-Masse.[30]

In Walt Whitman there is an earthy mysticism that Keir Hardie would have recognized from Robert Burns, but in this case, here is an urban man, a New Yorker, the "Proletarian Poet." In these few lines from part of *Leaves of Grass* entitled "Song of Myself," Whitman elevates sexual intercourse to sacramental heights:

> Divine am I inside and out, and I make holy whatever I touch or am touched from,
> The scent of these arm-pits aroma finer than prayer,
> This head more than churches, bibles and the creeds.[31]

The bold, explicitness of the imagery reveals a faith in humanity sharing the divine nature of the Creator, expressed most tangibly through sex. This is an egalitarianism of body, mind, and soul with moral, social, and political consequences, echoing the creed of his forebear Robert Burns. Hardie claimed to have worshipped at the shrine of Burns, though a report of a visit to his London apartment stated that Whitman and Emerson were honored by their statuettes on prominent display.[32] While we can appreciate the resonance between Burns and Whitman, it has to be acknowledged that Hardie

---

29. Whitman, *Complete Poems*, 22.
30. Whitman, *Complete Poems*, 37.
31. Whitman, *Complete Poems*, 87.
32. Fraser, "Keir Hardie," 113.

drew out threads from thinkers who contradicted one another in ideology and practice. His "big tent" concept of the labour movement meant that he wanted to recruit anyone who would bring further insight to the cause of human solidarity.

Interest in the radical dimensions of British and European history was stirred by several studies in the late nineteenth century from historians and social commentators who wanted to challenge the authorized versions of the past. Notable examples of published research were undertaken by Friedrich Engels, František Palacký, Tomáš Garrigue Masaryk, and Ernest Belfort Bax.[33] In his most comprehensive political treatise, *From Serfdom to Socialism*, Keir Hardie draws from the deep seams of radicalism to place his creed within a long and honorable tradition that both proclaimed and practiced a universal faith towards the liberation of all humanity. In the chapter entitled "Socialism and Christianity," Hardie writes about the godly egalitarianism of the Hebrew prophets, Jesus of Nazareth, and the early church, before continuing to tell the story of the religion of humanity as expressed through the Christian tradition. The radicalism of the tradition, he states, has been suppressed by the authorities of its official institutions.

> All this [radical Christian history], it may truly be said, is no evidence that Communism is the best form of Government, but it is evidence so strong as to be irrefutable that Christianity in its pristine purity had Communism as its invariable outcome, and that for nearly seventeen centuries the common people and their leaders believed Communism and Christianity to be synonymous terms. Incidentally, it shows how little modern churchgoers know of the history of their religion when they charge Socialism with being anti-Christian.[34]

According to Keir Hardie, "Christianity in its pristine purity" was practiced by the "weaving friars," who arrived in Britain from Europe in the thirteenth century. What distinguished the friars from other monastic orders was their rejection of retreating from

---

33. Callow, "Divine Discontent," 33.
34. Hardie, *From Serfdom*, 86.

the world; instead, they lived alongside the poorest and most marginalized of people, proclaiming the sacred universality of love, and supported themselves not by alms but through payment for manual labor and handicraft, such as weaving.[35] The medieval trade guild of Bruges is referred to by Hardie as a model of a communistic economic system.[36] While historians would have traditionally disputed Hardie's interpretation of the guild by emphasizing the exclusive nature of medieval guilds, more recent research has chimed with his view that they functioned as cooperative trading systems within feudal society.[37] When he turns his attention to the Peasants' Revolt in England and Europe, the English Civil War (or English Revolution) and the consequent Commonwealth under Oliver Cromwell, Keir Hardie identifies key figures for particular consideration. Emerson called for people to claim their humanity by being nonconformists, a cry proclaimed through the lives of John Ball, John Wycliffe, Thomas Müntzer, and Gerrard Winstanley. Hardie recalled these nonconformist leaders to write a people's history of true Christianity so that working men and women could be inspired by their example and creeds.

John Ball was a "hedge priest," an ordained minister who served outside of the official parish system at a time when the population of England had been reduced by almost half due to the Black Death and a poll tax was imposed upon them to pay for the war against France. Ball came to prominence in 1381, when his message of equality and freedom meant justice, and a fair distribution of wealth underpinned by a belief in human equality and solidarity became a significant factor in the instigation of the Peasants' Revolt across Essex and Kent.[38] Although Ball and other leaders, such as Wat Tyler, were executed and the revolt was suppressed, their message would endure for generations, inspired by a nonconformist spirit. A contemporary of John Ball was John Wycliffe, who was far from a "hedge priest," being an ordained theological

35. Hardie, *From Serfdom*, 84.
36. Hardie, *From Serfdom*, 84.
37. See Stabel, "Guilds."
38. Dunn, *Great Rising of 1381*, 60.

tutor at the University of Oxford and biblical translator. What he shared with Ball was condemnation of the privilege of the church and state institutions, and the desire to open Christianity to all people. For Wycliffe, the latter goal was sought through his translation of the Gospels into the vernacular, which he achieved in 1382. Wycliffe died in 1384, but his legacy was continued by the Lollard movement, which championed religious and social freedom. Wycliffe's writings inspired reformers like the Czech philosopher Jan Hus, whose execution in 1415 triggered a revolt about the nature of Christianity, leading to a Europe-wide conflict and further revolts from among the most oppressed people, most notably in Germany in 1524.[39]

While Wycliffe, via Hus, influenced the Protestant Reformation led by Martin Luther, John Calvin, and Huldrych Zwingli, which claimed the religious freedom of individuals, it was Thomas Müntzer who proved himself to be a nonconformist of nonconformists. A pivotal figure in the German Reformation and the history of European radicalism, Müntzer opposed Luther's compromise over feudal oppression, making him play a vital role in the peasant uprising of 1524–25. Another martyr of the cause, Müntzer attempted to realize the kingdom of God on earth by overturning society.[40] Then in his survey of radical Christian history, Keir Hardie looked forward to the following century and found inspiration in the leader of the True Levellers or Diggers, Gerrard Winstanley. During the English Civil Wars (1642–1651) and the subsequent Commonwealth (1649–1653) and Protectorate of Oliver and Richard Cromwell (1653–1659), numerous factions emerged with opposing objectives. The victory of the Parliamentarian forces led to hopes within certain quarters that a new era was dawning, which would mean liberation from the prevailing hierarchical, monarchist system. John Lilburne was the leader of the Agitators for egalitarian political reform, a group nicknamed the "Levellers" by opponents because of their campaign to level out legal rights across England. It was Lilburne's

---

39. Engels, "Peasant War in Germany," 10:428.

40. Scribner, *German Reformation*, 47.

support of maintaining ownership of private property that re-
sulted in the appearance of Winstanley and his "True Levellers"
who sought the abolition of property ownership. This group was
branded "Diggers" because they cultivated common land on St.
George's Hill, Surrey, in 1649.[41] In the pamphlet *The New Law of
Righteousness*, Winstanley returned to the example of the earliest
Christian community as recorded in the New Testament, when the
followers of Jesus "had all things in common" (Acts 2:44). After
the Restoration of Charles II in 1660, which shattered the dreams
of a godly egalitarian utopia, Winstanley continued to advocate
the redistribution of land through a communistic society and
proclaimed Christian universalism, reconciling all people in God,
the divinity of human solidarity. Winstanley claimed his humanity
through radical nonconformity, a heritage to which Keir Hardie
belonged and furthered. Peter Hill places Hardie in the tradition of
Ball, Müntzer, and Winstanley, writing for the *Communist Review*:

> Just as they spoke the language, and had the ways of
> thinking, of the dissenting chapels which had been such
> important centres of working-class life, so Hardie's Social-
> ism naturally expressed itself in terms of chapel oratory;
> which did not make his words any less militant.[42]

Through his great friendship with the former Salvation Army
officer and Labour activist Frank Smith, Keir Hardie encountered
Spiritualism. This religious movement grew in popularity in many
English-speaking countries during the late nineteenth century,
and it believes that it is possible to communicate with the spir-
its of dead people, who act as moral guides to the living. David
Howell, in his lecture marking the century since Hardie's death,
commented on Hardie's involvement with Spiritualism, stating
that its belief system and rituals "could be considered as democratic practice; within the séance, barriers of gender and class
could be transcended."[43] Hardie's son-in-law Emrys Hughes retells

---

41. Winstanley, *Common Treasury*, viii.
42. Hill, "Keir Hardie," 172.
43. Howell, "Hunting for the Real."

an amusing incident when Hardie attended a séance with Frank Smith and other friends, "when a spiritualist medium channelled historic figures such as Robert Burns, all of whom appealed to Keir Hardie to support the Irish Home Rule Bill."[44] Democratic practice was what Hardie sought from his religion of humanity, an all-embracing creed for universal solidarity and liberation.

As an international Labour leader, Hardie travelled widely and encountered many faith traditions along the way. He worked with Muslim socialists from Egypt,[45] and recorded his admiration of close Hindu-Muslim political cooperation on his visit to Benares in India.[46] In his contribution to the "Labour and Politics" lectures at Browning Hall in 1910, Hardie offered some reflections on Buddhism and Christianity, beginning with the statement, "All religions of the world have had for their object the attainment of peace in the human heart."[47] His comrade J. Bruce Glasier wrote in his memorial to Hardie of the attraction to the Bahá'í Faith,[48] a religion founded in 1863 by Bahá'u'lláh in Persia that teaches the equality and unity of all people and faiths.

> He had certainly given up all belief in the Christian Church as an exclusive means of Salvation. He could no more accept as true a religious dogma than a Socialist or political one that would exclude from the communion of citizens or saints, Jews, Freethinkers, Mohammedans [Muslims], Buddhists or people of any grade of enlightened, race or colour.[49]

Keir Hardie drew on the poetry of Robert Burns, the activism of radicals from the history of Britain and Europe, the insights of contemporary social commentators or prophets, and the knowledge of different world faith traditions to blend into a multi-textured religion of humanity that sought a godly egalitarianism.

44. Hughes, *Keir Hardie's Speeches*, 166.
45. Benn, *Keir Hardie*, 261.
46. Hardie, *India*, 122–23.
47. Ten Labour Members, *Labour and Religion*, 53.
48. Glasier, *J. Keir Hardie*, 70.
49. Glasier, *J. Keir Hardie*, 69.

For Hardie, true faith in the sacred cause towards the liberation and solidarity of all humanity was nondogmatic and inclusive, so his creed was fundamentally nonconformist in the fullest sense of the word. Just as his early days in the Evangelical Union had been an outcome of dissent, so his journey of faith from then on had avoided the compromises of institutional religion by discovering the truth on the margins of society and in the faith of those people outside of the official ranks of religious authorities. The poetry of Burns expressed something of the gritty worldview of ordinary working people, so it followed that his religion of humanity had to speak to the everyday realities of those same people, wherever in the world they were to be encountered. W. Hamish Fraser describes Hardie's religion as a "mixture of Christianity, transcendentalism and socialist theorising."[50] Here is a blended creed proclaiming the divinity of human solidarity, a creed that Keir Hardie began to realize as soon as he recognized that the cause to transform the lives of working-class communities is sacred.

50. Fraser, "Keir Hardie," 113.

5

Sacred Socialism

Workers of the world unite, wrote Karl Marx; you have
a world to win, and nothing to lose but your chains.
And they are uniting under the crimson banner of a
world-embracing principle which knows nor sect, nor
creed, nor race, and which offers new life and hope to
all created beings—the glorious Gospel of Socialism.[1]

CAROLINE BENN QUOTES from *Labour Leader*, when in January
1910 one of its articles looked back to Keir Hardie's reelection as member of parliament for Merthyr Tydfil in 1906, stating
that it was "not so much an election campaign as a crusade."[2] The
most nonconformist of politicians appealed to the dissenting chapel culture of South Wales, which honored the potential of every
person in the sight of God and forged tight-knit local communities of faith. Hardie's religiopolitical message about the dignity of
human worth and the need for cooperation to liberate working-class communities from poverty and oppression resonated with
the beliefs and aspirations of the Methodists, Baptists, and other
dissenters of the constituency. He reminded his constituents of

1. Hardie, *From Serfdom*, 124.
2. Benn, *Keir Hardie*, 257.

the godly egalitarianism envisioned by the Hebrew prophets and practiced by the early church, an insight into the kingdom of God on earth proclaimed in the gospel of Jesus and achievable by the Labour Party. Benn commented on the 1906 campaign, "Crusade is apt, for Hardie had the support of a local religious network, possibly his most important bulwark."[3] For Keir Hardie, socialism was the ultimate expression of his religion of humanity, the belief in the divinity of human solidarity. This chapter explores Hardie's relationship with two key socialist thinkers of his time: the father of international communism, Karl Marx, and the Arts and Crafts socialist, William Morris, men who offered vastly different visions to Hardie's "big tent" labour movement.

There are several references to Karl Marx in Keir Hardie's writings and speeches of the early twentieth century, indicating Hardie's awareness of the German philosopher who had been ex-iled in London for several decades until his death in 1883. Marx's most extensive work, the three-volume *Das Kapital*, was written during his exile, the British Museum Reading Room being the main location for his research.[4] With his background in the ratio-nalism of Hegelianism, which sought absolute idealism, the theory that being is ultimately comprehensible as an all-inclusive whole,[5] Marx developed his own social science. Marx placed class conflict as the means of understanding the evolution of all human soci-eties. Within his contemporary industrial, capitalist society, the conflict was between the bourgeoisie, who controlled the means of production, and the proletariat, who sold their labor for wages. Reflecting on how previous socioeconomic systems had imploded, Marx prophesied the self-destruction of capitalism, succeeded by socialism, which would lead to a classless, communist society.[6] Marx argued that a proletarian revolution would be the catalyst

3. Benn, *Keir Hardie*, 257.
4. Wheen, *Karl Marx*, 304.
5. Fischer, *Marx*, 18.
6. Fischer, *Marx*, 125.

for social change, hence his statement from *The Communist Manifesto*, which is misquoted by Keir Hardie at the beginning of this chapter,

> The Communists disdain to conceal their views and aims. They openly declare that their ends can be attained only by the forcible overthrow of all existing social conditions. Let the ruling classes tremble at a Communistic revolution. The proletarians have nothing to lose but their chains. They have a world to win—Working Men of All Countries, Unite![7]

During his visit to Lille in northern France, as part of the PSA Brotherhood delegation in May 1910, Keir Hardie cited Karl Marx alongside other European socialists as the condemners of ecclesiastical clericalism, which he argued was "the chief obstacle to the progress and development" of humankind.[8] The following year, Hardie published a tract entitled *Karl Marx: His Life and Message*, in which he adopts the founding father of international communism for the sacred cause of socialism. The suppression of Marx's Jewish heritage by the Christian authorities of the Prussian state was both acknowledged and condemned by Hardie,[9] before claiming the philosopher as a prophet whose message offered the most thorough, modern, scientific expression of an ancient creed.

> But is not, it may be asked, Socialism a revolutionary movement? Yes, no such revolutionary change has been conceived since the days 2,000 years ago, when John the Baptist called upon men to repent for the Kingdom of God was at hand! Socialism is revolutionary; it not only revolutionises the thoughts and actions of its adherents but also of the whole of society and the fabric of the State. Socialism is, without exception, the greatest revolutionary ideal which has ever fired the imagination, or enthused the heart of mankind. But, in the biting rebuke that Marx addressed to some of his professed followers,

7. See Marx and Engels, *Communist Manifesto*.
8. "Keir Hardie on Continent."
9. Hardie, *Karl Marx*, 4.

who would "substitute revolutionary phases for revolutionary evolution," we must be careful not to confuse the
end with the means. The Socialist state is the end, and
what concerns us most at present is the means by which
we are to get there. Marx only knew of one way; the organization of a working-class movement, which would in
process of time evolve the Socialist state. Socialism will
abolish the landlord class, the capitalist class, and the
working class. That is revolution; that the working class
by its action will one day abolish class distinctions.[10]

Despite Hardie's occasional references and the publication dedicated to the subject of Karl Marx, J. Bruce Glasier in his memorial
tribute to his comrade states, "I doubt if he ever read Marx or any
scientific exposition of Socialist theory."[11] It is also worth noting
that the bibliography of Keir Hardie's published works printed at
the end of Bruce Glasier's *A Memorial* does not refer to *Karl Marx:
His Life and Message* of 1911,[12] which seems strange because they
were both produced by the National Labour Press, the publishing
arm of the ILP. This indicates that Hardie's appreciation of Marx
did not fit into the post-Russian Revolution narrative of British
Labour politics of 1919. The theoretical Marxism of pre-1917 was
being tested by the particular interpretation and application of
Vladimir Ilyich Ulyanov (Lenin) in his formation of a Soviet Rus-
sia and Union, to the point that international socialists and social
democrats were holding their breaths as national communist parties were being formed and gaining strength in their societies.

Bruce Glasier's claim that Hardie had not flicked through the
pages of the slim *The Communist Manifesto*, never mind the hefty
Das Kapital, may be a reflection of his anti-Marxism;[13] but it is
given credence by the fact that Hardie's *Karl Marx: His Life and
Message* was actually an extensive review of John Spargo's book
Karl Marx: His Life and Work, first published in 1908. British-born

10. Hardie, *Karl Marx*, 15.
11. Glasier, *J. Keir Hardie*, 62.
12. Glasier, *J. Keir Hardie*, 84.
13. Thompson, *Enthusiasts*, 90.

Spargo emigrated to the United States in 1901 and became a significant figure in the American Left during the first two decades of the twentieth century. In his academically thorough biography, Spargo writes of his subject,

> His name rises like a great beacon in the modern world, a beacon which illumines millions of men and women in all the lands which capitalism has touched with its blight. He took the chaotic and despised elements of proletarian revolt and made them the greatest political movement in history. With a fidelity and whole-heartedness equalled only by his great genius and learning he served the working class and made its cause and its struggle his own.[14]

Previous to his review of Spargo's biography, Hardie had referred to Marx in very general terms, often grouping him within a pantheon of great contemporary socialists, such as claiming that the founders of the ILP and the British Labour Party were "in the direct line of apostolic succession from Marx and the other great mast minds of socialist theory and policy."[15] With Spargo, Hardie may have been engaging with Marxist theory secondhand, but he expresses an appreciation of its significance to the international labour movement, which is consistent with his belief in a broad, "big tent" labour movement, a broad alliance including Marxists, Fabians, trade unionists, and social democrats. Bruce Glasier notes Keir Hardie's attempts to bridge the ideological divisions, citing his attendance at both rival Marxist and Possibilist International Congresses in 1889, which both took place in Paris.[16] Hardie is clear in his praise of Marx's contribution to the sacred cause of socialism: "Little wonder that his memory is a consecrated treasure enshrined in the hearts of millions of the best men and women of all lands."[17]

In answer to the question during a socialist rally "Does Comrade Morris accept Marx's theory of value?" came the reply:

14. Spargo, *Karl Marx*, 352.

15. Hardie, *My Confession*, 16.

16. Glasier, *J. Keir Hardie*, 24.

17. Hardie, *Karl Marx*, 15.

> I am asked if I believe in Marx's theory of value. To speak
> frankly, I do not know what Marx's Theory of value is,
> and I'm damned if I want to know. . . . Truth to say, my
> friends, I have tried to understand Marx's theory but po-
> litical economy is not in my line, and much of it appears
> to be dreary rubbish. But I am, I hope, a Socialist none
> the less. It is enough political economy for me to know
> that the idle class is rich and the working class is poor,
> and that the rich are rich because they rob the poor.[18]

A giant of early British socialism alongside Keir Hardie, the reluc-
tance of William Morris to wrestle with the intricacies of socialist
theory was a source of frustration for Marxists who poured over
every word of the collected works of Marx and Engels. In their
Communist Manifesto of 1848, there were cautionary comments
about what they described as "Reactionary Socialisms" including
"Feudal Socialism": "half lamentation, half lampoon; half echo of
the past, half menace of the future . . . through total incapacity to
comprehend the march of modern history."[19] While Morris may
have objected to the critical tone, he would not have denied that
his socialism was based on a radical tradition gleaned from his
appreciation of the past.

By the time Morris came to write his socialist novel *News from
Nowhere* (subtitled *Being Some chapters from a Utopian Romance*),
originally serialized in the Socialist League's journal *Commonweal*
in 1890, he had established himself as a writer of Romantic poems
and tales, among his many other achievements. Inspired by the
writings of William Chaucer and the arts, crafts, and architecture
of the Middle Ages, along with the folklore of northern Europe,
Morris wrote about earthly paradises with gallant knights and their
epic quests, most often set in an idealized medieval England. In
his introduction to a collection of Morris's early romances, Alfred
Noyes writes, "His Utopias of the past, though he projected them
into the future, were in many of their aspects hardly more than a

18. Glasier, *William Morris*, 32.
19. Keating, *Victorian Prophets*, 137.

lyrical cry for his own dead days."[20] Such words reflect the nature of *News from Nowhere*, the tale of a Victorian socialist called William Guest, who wakes from sleep one day into the egalitarian society of 2102, where the horrors of capitalism and industrialization have been replaced with the joys of the emancipation and rewards of a pastoral idyll. In the story, society altered its course through "the change,"[21] a rapid movement of downtrodden and disillusioned urban dwellers to reclaim the land, lifestyle, and traditions of the rural villages.

> This is how we stand. England was once a country of clearings amongst the woods and wastes, with a few towns interspersed, which were fortresses for the feudal army, markets for the folk, gathering places for the craftsmen. It then became a country of huge and foul workshops and fouler gambling-dens, surrounded by an ill-kept, poverty-stricken farm, pillaged by the masters of the workshops. It is now a garden, where nothing is wasted and nothing is spoilt, with the necessary dwellings, sheds, and workshops scattered up and down the country, all trim and neat and pretty. For, indeed, we should be too much ashamed of ourselves if we allowed the making of goods, even on a large scale, to carry with it the appearance, even, of desolation and misery.[22]

William Morris, "poet, artist, manufacturer and socialist,"[23] was a leading figure in the Arts and Crafts movement, promoting traditional craftsmanship as opposed to industrial manufacturing, and advocating economic and social reform. The movement often used a style of decoration that was inspired by medieval design, thus encouraging the reclamation of skills being lost in an industrialized society where the machine replaced individual craftsmanship. As a student at Oxford University in the early 1850s, Morris joined Edward Burne-Jones and others to form the Brotherhood,

---

20. Noyes, *Early Romances*, xvi.

21. Morris, *News from Nowhere*, 104.

22. Morris, *News from Nowhere*, 105.

23. Noyes, *Early Romances*, xi.

or Birmingham Set, who brought together their passion for Romantic literature with a commitment to the welfare of society.[24] The turning point for this group of undergraduates came when they read the social criticism of John Ruskin, which stated that the morality and welfare of society were related to the qualities of its architecture and the nature of its work. According to Burne-Jones, who would go on to found the Pre-Raphaelite fellowship of artists, the Brotherhood of idealist Oxford students set out to "wage Holy warfare against the age."[25] During the 1860s and 1870s, Morris established and grew a decorative arts company, which set the style and standard for what became the Arts and Crafts movement. By the 1870s, he was associated with radical liberalism to address the social and economic needs of an increasingly industrialized and urban society. Morris became a founding member of the Radical Union in 1881, but soon rejected the radical wing of liberalism for socialism, and in 1883 he joined Henry Hyndman's Democratic Federation.[26] Mounting tensions with Hyndman over his authoritarian leadership led Morris and several other leading members of what had become the Social Democratic Federation (SDF), to form the Socialist League in December 1884.[27]

Tony Wright in his introduction to socialist theories writes, "William Morris sought to integrate Marxist ideas with a Ruskinian tradition of aesthetic protest against the civilization of commercial capitalism."[28] Such integration was not out of step with many of the pioneers of early British socialism of the 1880s and the first few years of the following decade. Morris's writing played an important role in Keir Hardie's formative period within the labour movement. John Callow reflects on the important influence of the Arts and Crafts socialist on Hardie's thought and politics: "Hardie sees Marxism as being an organic part of an indigenous radical political tradition that found its fullest expression in the life and

24. Naylor, *Arts and Crafts Movement*, 96–97.
25. Naylor, *Arts and Crafts Movement*, 97.
26. MacCarthy, *William Morris*, 467.
27. MacCarthy, *William Morris*, 504.
28. Wright, *Socialisms*, 9.

career of William Morris."[29] Hardie emphasizes the significance of Morris when he writes in 1907 about the tradition of Jesus the Communist being reignited in Britain throughout the nineteenth century:

> When Capitalism was in process of converting England into a veritable hell, it was Robert Owen the Communist who gave his fortune and his life in an effort to save her people from destruction. When the hell had been made and the Chartist movement was in full swing, its leaders were socialists almost to a man, as had been those of the Radical movement before them. It was fear of socialism much more than of Radicalism which led to the Peterloo massacre. When Radicalism with its arid gospel of self-ishness was blatant with the joy of triumph, the impos-ing form of William Morris the Communist stood lonely and grand like a beacon on a mighty rock in the midst of a storm-tossed sea warning the people of England of the danger towards which they were heading.[30]

Where Hardie did not follow the light of Morris's beacon was along the route away from parliamentary politics. William Morris advocated a decentralized, self-governing form of associational so-cialism, having rejected both revolutionary and reformist versions of state socialism.[31] A diary entry from 1887 reveals that there was pressure by Fabian and SDF members to direct the Socialist League towards engaging with the electoral system, but Morris is clear that for him such a step "would be a misfortune."[32]

The reference points for Morris's socialism predated modern democracy, harking back to a romanticized time of close-knit communities and craft guilds, an image that appealed to Hardie, though he sought parliamentary representation to achieve his political goals. For both pioneers of British socialism, their poli-tics was the most recent manifestation of a long, sacred tradition that sought solidarity and liberation. Serialized in *Commonweal*

29. Callow, "Divine Discontent," 27.

30. Hardie, *From Serfdom*, 123.

31. Wright, *Socialisms*, 80.

32. Boos, *William Morris' Socialist Diary*, 97.

between November 13, 1886, and January 22, 1887, *A Dream of John Ball* is a clear indication of William Morris claiming heritage for his politics. Like *News from Nowhere* several years later, time travel is the literary device used to tell the tale, but in *A Dream of John Ball*, the narrator journeys back to Kent during the Peasants' Revolt of 1381 to encounter the "hedgerow priest" John Ball. The dialogue between priest and time traveler reveals their shared faith in the universal religion of humanity, expressed most clearly in socialism, declaring the divinity of human solidarity: "John Ball, be of good cheer; for once more thou knowest, as I know, that the Fellowship of Men shall endure, however many tribulations it may have to wear through."[33]

Keir Hardie held a "big tent" view of the labour movement, and by doing so was able to recruit a wide range of historical and contemporary figures to his crusade. Both the appendix and bibliography of *From Serfdom to Socialism* reveal the broadness of his ranks, as Hardie quotes from Ruskin, Mill, Kropotkin, Mohammed, and St. Ambrose, and draws attention to the writings of Marx, Morris, Hyndman, and Henry George. For Hardie, Karl Marx gave a thorough, scientific underpinning to socialist thought, making him the socialist prophet of the future, while William Morris was a socialist prophet who rooted it into the rich radicalism of British history. Socialism was the ultimate expression of his religion of humanity, declaring the divinity of human solidarity. What Keir Hardie traces in the theories and ideals of all the people he references in his speeches and writings is a common thread stretching back to the Hebrew prophets, Jesus of Nazareth, and the early church: the gospel of socialism about universal kinship fulfilled by an egalitarian agenda, making the struggle to realize this goal a sacred cause.

> The Holy Alliance which Socialism is achieving is not that of crowned heads but of horny hands, and therein lies the only real hope of peace on earth.[34]

33. Morris, *News from Nowhere*, 36.
34. Hardie, *From Serfdom*, 132.

Conclusion

Keir Hardie's Creed

> Socialism with its promise of freedom, its larger hope
> for humanity, its triumph of peace over war, its binding
> of the races of the earth into one all-embracing brother-
> hood, must prevail. Capitalism is the creed of the dying
> present; Socialism throbs with the life of the days that
> are to be.[1]

THE ORIGIN OF KEIR HARDIE's creed predates his acceptance
of the Christian faith and his involvement in the temperance
movement. His core belief, around which he would weave a religion
of humanity, came from the drudgery and oppression experienced
in childhood and in an upbringing, though labelled "nonreligious," that held to equality and self-worth, the consequence of
which was a heightened sensitivity to hypocrisy. The theological
foundation of the Evangelical Union gave Hardie a concept of
God that emphasized the egalitarianism of grace personified in
Jesus. Later influenced by Ernest Renan and R. J. Campbell, Keir
Hardie regarded the incarnation as an event or demonstration of
sacred solidarity with the whole of creation, making the laborer
and political agitator Jesus of Nazareth the epitome of the divine
in human kinship.

1. Hardie, *From Serfdom*, 139.

What Jesus represented was broadened socially, politically, and economically in his gospel of the kingdom of God on earth as taught throughout the Sermon on the Mount. In these teachings, Hardie found both a vision and a program for a new world order of universal solidarity, where justice and peace reigned. He traced a common thread through the prophetic tradition, the early church communities, and the radical Christian activists of British and European history. Hardie found it also in the poetry of Robert Burns and Walt Whitman, the social commentary of contemporary "prophets," and the insights of world faiths. The common denominator was godly egalitarianism, as a concept and in practice. Although Hardie was drawing on a broad, and sometimes inconsistent, range of ideologies, what brought them together for him was their nonconformity, a dissenting spirit that returned Hardie to his core values of equality and self-worth. By the last decade of his life, Hardie had expanded his religion of humanity beyond the conventional beliefs of Christianity, and by doing so, he could grasp a universal creed that proclaimed the divinity of human solidarity. The ultimate expression of this religion of humanity, and the only means to its fulfilment, was socialism through the international labour movement. With Keir Hardie, the movement was a "big tent" welcoming all who were committed to its sacred cause.

Keir Hardie's life ended in tragedy. The First World War represented the evil of human division, the antithesis of his heartfelt beliefs and hopes. The sacred cause to which Hardie had dedicated his life seemed to be facing absolute defeat, so he spent the final year of his life feeling totally disillusioned as his vision and values were discredited by the words and actions of politicians and their military commanders in Britain, Europe, and across the world. Though tributes were paid after Hardie's death to his faithful compassion and dedication to campaigns to alleviate poverty and injustice, many of these homages were muted due to the jingoistic atmosphere in which they were uttered. Only when the deadly cost of the war was realized was there an appreciation of what Hardie had stood for and the potency of his creed. By the end of the decade, he was being reassessed and regarded as a prophet of peace, justice, and universal kinship.

The tracing of James Keir Hardie's influences, inspirations, and insights has been a legitimate task because it breaks new ground in our appreciation of the man and his central beliefs. Yet, any attempt to draft out his creed would fly in the face of Hardie's non-dogmatism, both politically and theologically. But to define his faith is to stand in line with commentators during Keir Hardie's lifetime and his biographers since, all of whom have written their analysis, interpretation, and summary of Hardie's views and values. With the recognition of the task's dichotomy, what follows is a composite statement or "creed" based on Keir Hardie's speeches, newspaper articles, and other publications. Some of the references date back to the 1890s, but most are from the last ten years of his life, offering both an overview and the maturity of his thought. So, being prepared for the wrath of Keir Hardie, here is my attempt at collating his creed:

> *Socialism is the Christianity of today,[2]*
> *the purest expression of the politics of the kingdom of God on earth[3]*
> *as taught by Jesus of Nazareth, worker, agitator, revolutionary, friend and savior of the poor and oppressed.[4]*
> *Socialism is the promise of hope and freedom for the whole of humanity,*
> *the triumph of peace over war,*
> *it eradicates poverty by abolishing private property*
> *and binds the peoples of the world into an all-embracing kinship.[5]*
> *Socialism is the gospel of the whole labour movement,[6]*
> *being not only a good system of political economy*
> *but also a philosophy of life that is altogether beautiful,*

2. "Religion and Labour."
3. "Christianity and Twentieth Century."
4. "Keir Hardie on Continent."
5. Hardie, *From Serfdom*, 139.
6. Hardie, *My Confession*, 14.

based on love, fraternity, and service.[7]
Socialism is a sacred cause,[8]
making the labour movement a true "broad church" of the universal religion of humanity,[9]
proclaiming the divinity of human solidarity.[10]

What is the relevance of this study for contemporary politics and faith? To state that solidarity is of paramount importance for the future of our world is a declaration about three interrelated matters: interdependence, internationalism, inclusivity.

At the height of the COVID-19 pandemic, the European Union published an article that stated that international solidarity was crucial in addressing the emergency: "No country, no matter how big, can resolve this global crisis on its own."[11] Faced with an unprecedented worldwide crisis came the realization that we need one another as human beings. A recent report from the United Nations about the current international refugee emergency outlined the causes of the situation: "War, human rights violations, underdevelopment, climate change and natural disasters are leading more people to leave their homes than at any time since we have had reliable data."[12] The report continues, "But this is not a crisis of numbers; it is a crisis of solidarity."[13] A doctrine of individual self-worth and self-reliance is false without the qualification that our agency relies on the affirmation and opportunities granted to us by a just, human society. In an encyclical letter about the nature of fraternity and international social friendship entitled *Fratelli Tutti*, Pope Francis writes,

> Each of us is fully a person when we are part of a people; at the same time, there are no people without respect for the individuality of each person. "People" and "person"

7. "Editorial" (1896).
8. Ten Labour Members, *Labour and Religion*, 54.
9. "Religion and Labour Movement."
10. "Mr Hardie MP in Manchester."
11. Borrell, "Solidarity Is Essential."
12. United Nations, "Refugees and Migrants."
13. United Nations, "Refugees and Migrants."

are corrective terms. Nonetheless, there are attempts nowadays to reduce persons to isolated individuals easily manipulated by powers pursuing spurious interests. Good politics will seek ways of building communities at every level of social life, to recalibrate and reorient globalization and thus avoid its disruptive effects.[14]

My own Christian denomination, the Methodist Church in Britain, has affirmed its responsibility to be an increasingly inclusive church: "We are committed to becoming a church that prioritises justice and dignity for all, especially those who have previously been excluded, and which stands in active solidarity with them."[15]

Our interdependence goes beyond us as a species. As human beings, we will not survive without rebalancing our relationship with our natural environment or created order. It is dawning on an increasing number of the world's population that due to the corrosive impact of industrialization, we have reached a tipping point in terms of the sustainability of our planet. Just as Keir Hardie championed the urgent issues of his time, including women's suffrage and the challenge to the authority of the British Empire over its colonies, that same spirit of dissent is felt today in many struggles, such as the environmental and racial justice movements. From the radical wing of environmentalism comes this vision statement produced by XR UK, the British expression of Extinction Rebellion:

> Our world is in crisis. Life itself is under threat. Yet every crisis contains the possibility of transformation. Across the world, heralded by the young, people are waking up and coming together.
>
> We hear history calling to us from the future. We catch glimpses of a new world of love, respect, and regeneration, where we have restored the intricate web of all life. It's a future that's inside us all—located in the fierce love we carry for our children, in our urge to help a stranger

14. Francis, *Fratelli Tutti*, 73.
15. Methodist Church, *Working Towards*, 1.

in distress, in our wish to forgive, even when that seems too much to ask.

And so we rebel for this, calling in joy, creativity and beauty. We rise in the name of truth and withdraw our consent for ecocide, oppression, and patriarchy. We rise up for a world where power is shared for regeneration, repair and reconciliation. We rise for love in its ultimate wisdom. Our vision stretches beyond our own lifespan, to a horizon dedicated to future generations and the restoration of our planet's integrity.

Together, our rebellion is the gift this world needs. We are XR and you are us.[16]

In a post-Brexit, COVID-19–recovering Britain, the issue of the dismantling of the United Kingdom is back on the national, political agenda because of the decisions made by the English electorate and their politicians. It is contested by both sides of the argument as to where Keir Hardie would have stood on the issue of Scottish independence, because after his commitment to Scottish trade unionism and the founding of the Scottish Labour Party, he concentrated on the British political scene, representing constituencies in London and South Wales. The leader of the Welsh Labour Party and First Minister of Wales, Mark Drakeford, has argued that the future of the United Kingdom as a political entity depends on it becoming a "solidarity union" of devolved nations.[17] The whole concept of a European Union (EU) based on socialist principles was a dream Hardie cherished as part of an internationalist program, so what he would have made of the EU is a matter of speculation, reflecting the debate within the British Labour Party about its position during the referendum and its aftermath. But it can be stated that a creed based on human solidarity will seek opportunities for cooperation and comradeship.

The League of Nations emerged from the trauma of the First World War, which Hardie would have welcomed, though

16. See https://extinctionrebellion.uk/the-truth/about-us/.
17. Carrell, "UK Could Break Up."

scrutinizing its aims and principles; similarly the current United Nations, an international response to the Second World War. The Russian invasion of Ukraine in February 2022 and the subsequent war have tested the foundation of transnational agreements and alliances. Both NATO (North Atlantic Treaty Organization) and the EU have openly supported Ukraine against Russian aggression, but, while the armed conflict continues, the extent of the solidarity has fallen short of accepting Ukraine's membership of both alliances because of the consequences for wider global stability. While pernicious maneuvering is at play on the world stage, from the belief held by Keir Hardie's creed, any threat to international cooperation that hinders working towards peace, justice, and greater kinship must be condemned as a denial of our shared humanity and its sacredness.

The COVID-19 pandemic shone a bright light on inequality and injustice in our societies. Although key workers were praised for their contributions to the welfare of nations around the world, most of those workers were from ethnic minorities and other economically oppressed communities in their societies, and they were the most vulnerable to the virus. Within that global atmosphere and enraged by examples of police brutality leading to numerous preventable deaths, including that of George Floyd in Minneapolis on May 25, 2020, the Black Lives Matter movement became an international force for justice. The organization has highlighted the barriers facing people of color across the world.[18] Black Lives Matter is founded on the principle of liberation through solidarity:

> We are expansive. We are a collective of liberators who believe in an inclusive and spacious movement. We also believe that in order to win and bring as many people with us along the way, we must move beyond the narrow nationalism that is all too prevalent in Black communities. We must ensure we are building a movement that brings all of us to the front.
>
> We affirm the lives of Black queer and trans folks, disabled folks, undocumented folks, folks with records,

18. British Future, "Beyond BAME."

women, and all Black lives along the gender spectrum. Our network centers those who have been marginalized within Black liberation movements.

We are working for a world where Black lives are no longer systematically targeted for demise.

We affirm our humanity, our contributions to this society, and our resilience in the face of deadly oppression.

The call for Black lives to matter is a rallying cry for *all* Black lives striving for liberation.[19]

Keir Hardie was committed to parliamentary democracy as a socialist. He fought for universal suffrage to gain for all men and women inclusion and representation within the electoral system so that their voices could be heard at every level of social governance. Research into the women's suffrage movement of early twentieth-century Britain has revealed the vital role played by women from marginalized communities, notably queer, black, and disabled.[20] People suffering from what is increasingly appreciated to be intersectional oppression have united at key moments in history to struggle together for common rights and freedom. The international labour movement must champion intersectional justice to ensure that issues of ethnicity, age, ability, faith, sexuality, gender identity, and economic class are no longer fault lines but springboards towards a world living for mutual freedom, solidarity, and equality.[21]

While he embraced a "big tent" concept of the labour movement in appreciation of the insights of a wide variety of socialists, social democrats, and other labour activists whose political agendas ranged from class revolution to craft guilds, Hardie's preference was socialism through the reach of a "big state." From the perspective of his creed, a society founded on the principle of human solidarity would care, resource, and empower all its citizens by guaranteeing high standards of service through the

19. See https://blacklivesmatter.com/about/ (emphasis original).
20. Braidwood, "Queer, Disabled, and Women."
21. See https://www.intersectionaljustice.org/what-is-intersectionality.

nationalization of all healthcare, welfare, education, utilities, and public transport. A society based on the spirit of Hardie's creed would eradicate poverty and homelessness through a fair tax system covering both corporate and personal income, introduce a just welfare system, build social housing, create a culture of fulfilment through employment as a positive contribution to one another, and ensure "cradle to grave" support of a freely accessible health service. Such a society would be a safe haven for asylum seekers and refugees, expressing the nation's commitment to international solidarity with all persecuted and marginalized people.

Whenever we witness the weaponization of ethnic, racial, gender, and regional differences by politicians and social movements; and whenever the fear of the foreigner, the "enemy within," or "the other" is used to justify racism, oppression, and injustice, only social and political alliances based on faith in human solidarity can offer resilience, resistance, and resolution.[22] Such faithful people can be drawn from the world's religious communities and different ideological traditions when they recognize that their cause is a shared struggle for the common good. The politics of hatred and fear shout loudly for various ways of achieving ethnic cleansing, thought control, and heightened security, all in the name of defending democracy and freedom. The cry for the end of what is described as "cancel culture" and the growth of the so-called "Woke" mentality is a contemporary manifestation, in populist form, of the politics of hate. With his lifelong struggle for the liberation of people from marginalized and oppressed communities, today Keir Hardie would be labelled by some as Woke. In light of Hardie's struggle, and clearly expressed through his creed, the term *Woke* would probably be embraced by the Labour pioneer as he claimed it for the sacred cause of socialism, redeeming the word to mean those people who are awake to injustice.

The introductory chapter began with a quotation from the secularist social reformer, G. W. Foote, who questioned Keir Hardie's faith. Foote stated that if Hardie accepted "the supernatural

22. Tisdall, "Europe's Lurch."

part of the Gospels,"[23] which he defined as the miracles, incarnation, and resurrection of Jesus, then that would prove to him that Keir Hardie was a Christian. But this prophetic pioneer of the British labour movement was not about scoring points to prove his worth and the depth of his convictions. Instead, pivotal to Hardie's faith in socialism, and the core of his creed, is that Jesus of Nazareth, the worker, agitator, and friend and savior of people facing poverty and oppression, reveals incarnation to be the sign of sacred solidarity with humanity and all of creation. Keir Hardie discovered for himself that across the centuries and throughout the world, the struggle for liberation had been pursued by people inspired by their values and beliefs from many faith traditions and philosophies of thought: labour history is religious history.

> The work of the labour movement today is to apply those principles of Christ's teaching to modern industrial and economic problems so as to bring about the time when there shall be no poverty, either of body, mind of spirit, but in a land, in a world so beautiful, so richly endowed, that there shall be abundance for all . . .[24]

---

23. Foote, *Flowers of Freethought*, 164.
24. Ten Labour Members, *Labour and Religion*, 55.

Bibliography

Ballinger, Steve. "Beyond 'BAME': What Does the Public Think?" British Future, Mar. 29, 2021. https://www.britishfuture.org/beyond-bame-what-does-the-public-think/#:~:text=Across%20the%20public%20as%20a,being%20sure%20of%20its%20meaning.

Benn, Caroline. *Keir Hardie: A Biography*. London: Hutchinson, 1992.

Borrell, Josep. "Solidarity Is Essential in the Face of an Unprecedented Global Crisis." European Union External Action, June 26, 2020. https://www.eeas.europa.eu/eeas/solidarity-essential-face-unprecedented-global-crisis_en.

Boos, Florence S. *William Morris' Socialist Diary*. 2nd ed. Nottingham, UK: Five Leaves, 2018.

Braidwood, Ella. "The Queer, Disabled, and Women of Color Suffragettes History Forgot." *Vice*, Feb. 5, 2018. https://www.vice.com/en/article/9kz54p/uk-suffrage-centenary-anniversary-women-color-queer-disabled-activists.

Brockway, A. Fenner. "James Keir Hardie (1856–1915)." In *Christian Social Reformers of the Nineteenth Century*, edited by Hugh Martin, 227–42. London: SCM, 1933. First published 1927.

Burns, J. H., and H. L. A. Hart, eds. *A Comment on the Commentaries* and *A Fragment on Government*. By Jeremy Bentham. The Collected Works of Jeremy Bentham. London: Athlone, 1971.

Burns, Robert. *The Complete Poems and Songs of Robert Burns*. Glasgow: Waverley, 2011.

Callow, John. "A Divine Discontent: Keir Hardie and the Genesis of British Socialism." In *From Serfdom to Socialism*, by James Keir Hardie et al., 11–48. London: Lawrence and Wishart, 2015. First published 1907.

Calvin, John. *Institutes of the Christian Religion, 1536 Edition*. Grand Rapids: Eerdmans, 1994.

Campbell, R. J. *The New Theology*. London: Chapman and Hall, 1907.

———. *The New Theology and the Socialist Movement*. Stockport, UK: Socialist, 1908.

———. *New Theology Sermons*. London: Williams and Norgate, 1907.

———. "Rev R J Campbell's Tribute." *Nottingham Journal*, Sept. 30, 1915.

Carlyle, Thomas. *Sartor Resartus: Lectures on Heroes. Chartism. Past and Present.* London: Chapman and Hall, 1888.

Carrell, Severin. "UK Could Break Up Unless It Is Rebuilt as 'Solidarity Union,' Says Mark Drakeford." *Guardian*, May 29, 2023. https://www.theguardian.com/politics/2023/may/29/uk-could-break-up-unless-it-is-rebuilt-as-solidarity-union-says-mark-drakeford.

Ceresko, Anthony R. *Introduction to the Old Testament: A Liberation Perspective.* Maryknoll, NY: Orbis, 1992.

Chalamet, Christophe. *Revivalism and Social Christianity: The Prophetic Faith of Henri Nick and André Troemé.* Eugene, OR: Pickwick, 2013.

"Christianity and the Twentieth Century." *Leigh Chronicle & Weekly District Advertiser,* June 3, 1910.

"The Clergy and the ILP." *Labour Leader*, Aug. 18, 1905.

Conway, Katharine St. John, and J. Bruce Glasier. *The Religion of Socialism: Two Aspects.* Manchester, UK: Labour, n.d. [1890s].

Corbyn, Jeremy. "Afterword: Keir Hardie and 21st Century Socialism." In *Keir Hardie and 21st Century Socialism*, edited by Pauline Bryan, 182–84. Edinburgh: Luath, 2019.

Cruddas, Jon. "Keir Hardie's Ethical Socialism." *Oxford Left Review* 2 (May 2010) 16–22.

Dagon, Jane Victoria. "Ernest Renan and the Question of Race." PhD diss., Louisiana State University, 1999.

Dunn, Alastair. *The Great Rising of 1381.* Stroud, UK: Tempus, 2002.

Edwards, Wil Jon. *From the Valley I Came.* London: Angus and Robertson, 1956.

Emerson, Ralph Waldo. *Self-Reliance and Other Essays.* New York: Dover, 1993.

Engels, Friedrich. "The Peasant War in Germany." In *The Collected Works of Karl Marx and Friedrich Engels*, 10:397–482. New York: International, 1978.

Fischer, Ernst. *Marx in His Own Words.* Harmondsworth, UK: Penguin, 1973.

Foote, G. W. *Flowers of Freethought.* 2nd ser. London: Forder, 1894.

Foster, Dawn. "Love Thy Neighbour." *Tribune* (Winter 2019) 62–63.

Francis, Pope. *Fratelli Tutti: Encyclical Letter on Fraternity and Social Friendship.* Rome: Vaticana, 2020.

Fraser, W. Hamish. "Keir Hardie: Radical, Socialist, Feminist." *Études écossaises* [Scottish studies] 10 (2005) 103–15.

Fyfe, Hamilton. *Keir Hardie.* Great Lives Series. London: Duckworth, 1935.

Gill, Peter. "National Coal Strike." Apr. 23, 2008. https://web.archive.org/web/20120920172933/http://dspace.dial.pipex.com/town/parade/abj76/PG/pieces/lawrence/national_coal_strike.shtml.

Glasier, J. Bruce. *J. Keir Hardie: A Memorial.* Manchester, UK: National Labour, 1919.

———. *Keir Hardie: The Man and His Message.* London: Independent Labour Party, 1919.

———. *William Morris and the Early Days of the Socialist Movement.* London: Longmans, 1921.

Gore, Charles. "Introduction." In *The Life of Jesus,* by Ernest Renan, ix–xvii. London: Dent and Sons Limited, 1927. First published 1863.

Hardie, J. Keir. *Can a Man Be a Christian on a Pound a Week?* Revised 5th ed. London: Independent Labour Party, 1905. First published 1901.

———. "Comments on Attending Wilson Barrett's Play *The Sign of the Cross* at the Lyric Theatre, London, March 1896." In *Keir Hardie's Speeches and Writings: From 1888 to 1915,* edited by Emrys Hughes, 54. Glasgow: Forward, c. 1925.

———. "Editorial." *Labour Leader,* Nov. 28, 1896.

———. "Editorial." *Labour Leader,* Feb. 17, 1900.

———. "Editorial." *Labour Leader,* Jan. 22, 1909.

———. "An Open Letter to the Clergy." *Labour Leader,* June 23, 1905.

———. *From Serfdom To Socialism.* London: Lawrence and Wishart, 2015. First published 1907.

———. *The ILP—All Out It.* Manchester, UK: National Labour, 1909.

———. *India: Impressions and Suggestions.* 2nd ed. London: Independent Labour Party, 1909.

———. *Karl Marx: His Life and Message.* Manchester, UK: National Labour, 1911.

———. *My Confession of Faith in the Labour Alliance.* London: ILP, 1909.

Harvie, Christopher, and H. C. G. Matthew. *Nineteenth-Century Britain: A Very Short Introduction.* Oxford: Oxford University Press, 2000.

Heschel, Susannah. *The Aryan Jesus: Christian Theologians and the Bible in Nazi Germany.* Princeton, NJ: Princeton University Press, 2008.

Hill, Peter. "Keir Hardie." *Communist Review* (June 1948) 172–78.

Holman, Bob. *Keir Hardie: Labour's Greatest Hero?* Oxford: Lion, 2010.

Howell, David. "Hunting for the Real Keir Hardie." Independent Labour, Apr. 8, 2016. https://www.independentlabour.org.uk/2016/04/08/hunting-for-the-real-keir-hardie/.

Hughes, Emrys. *Keir Hardie.* London: Allen & Unwin, 1956.

———, ed. *Keir Hardie's Speeches and Writings: From 1888 to 1915.* Glasgow: Forward, ca. 1925.

Inglis, K. S. *Churches and the Working Classes in Victorian England.* London: Routledge and Kegan, 1963.

Johnson, Francis. *Keir Hardie's Socialism.* London: Independent Labour Party, 1922.

Johnson, Neil. *The Labour Church: The Movement and Its Message.* London: Routledge, 2018.

Josephus, Flavius. *Antiquities of the Jews 18.* In *Jerusalem and Rome: The Writings of Josephus,* edited by Nahum N. Glatzer, 146. London: Collins/Fontana, 1966. First published 1960.

Keating, Peter. *The Victorian Prophets: A Reader from Carlyle to Wells.* Glasgow: Collins Sons/Fontana, 1981.

"Keir Hardie on the Continent." *Labour Leader,* June 3, 1910.

"Keir Hardie's Religion." *Dundee Evening Telegraph,* Oct. 1, 1915.

Kenworthy, John C. "J. Keir Hardie, M.P.: Men of the Movement." *Labour Leader*, June 30, 1894.

Killingray, David. "The Pleasant Sunday Afternoon Movement: Revival in the West Midlands, 1875–90?" *Studies in Church History* 44 (2008) 262–74.

Kirsch, Charles E. "Theology of James Morison, with Special Reference to His Theories of the Atonement." PhD diss., University of Edinburgh, 1939.

Knox, W. W. "Religion and the Scottish Labour Movement c. 1900–39." *Journal of Contemporary History* 23 (Oct. 1988) 609–30.

"Lord Overtoun." *Labour Leader*, Jan. 1899.

"Lord Overtoun. Mr Lorimer Observes Silence. The Session Take Action." *Dundee Courier*, July 10, 1899.

MacCathy, Fiona. *William Morris: A Life for Our Time*. London: Faber and Faber, 1994.

Marx, Karl, and Friedrich Engels. *The Communist Manifesto*. Adapted by Martin Rowson. London: SelfMadeHero, 2018.

Maxton, James. *Keir Hardie, Pioneer and Prophet*. London: Johnson/National Labour, 1933.

McArthur Conner, J. *Jas. Keir Hardie's Life Story: From Pit Trapper to Parliament*. London: Forgotten, 2018. First published 1917.

McLean, Iain. *Keir Hardie*. London: Allen Lane, 1975.

Methodist Church. *Working Towards a Fully Inclusive Methodist Church*. Manchester, UK: Trustees for Methodist Church Purposes, 2023.

Mill, John Stuart. *On Liberty*. London: Routledge and Sins, 1924. First published 1859.

Miranda, José P. *Communism in the Bible*. London: SCM, 1982.

Morgan, Kenneth O. *Keir Hardie: Radical and Socialist*. London: Phoenix Giants, 1997. First published 1975.

———. *Labour People: Leaders and Lieutenants, Hardie to Kinnock*. Oxford: Oxford University Press, 1987.

Morris, William. *News from Nowhere and Other Writings*. London: Penguin, 2004.

"Mr Hardie MP in Manchester." *Manchester Courier and Lancashire General Advertiser*, Jan. 22, 1894.

"Mr Keir Hardie and the Congregationalists. Do the Churches Heed the Poor? Councillor Beavan and a Dissenting Deacon say 'No.'" *Western Mail*, Oct. 17, 1892.

"Mr Keir Hardie at Mansfield House." *Stratford Express*, Apr. 2, 1892.

"Mr Keir Hardie at the Labour Church." *Cumberland & Westmorland Herald*, May 13, 1893.

"Mr Keir Hardie MP and the Congregational Union." *Morning Post*, Oct. 12, 1892.

"Mr Keir Hardie MP and the Labour Church." *Birmingham Daily Post*, Oct. 9, 1893.

"Mr Keir Hardie MP at Dowlais." *Merthyr Pioneer*, Mar. 3, 1912.

"Mr Keir Hardie MP in Cardiff." *Western Daily Mercury*, Apr. 6, 1912.

"Mr Keir Hardie MP in Cheltenham." *Cheltenham Examiner*, Feb. 29, 1912.

"Mr Keir Hardie's Confession." *South Wales Daily News*, May 16, 1910.

Naylor, Gillian. *The Arts and Crafts Movement: A Study of Its Sources, Ideals and Influence on Design Theory*. London: Studio Vista, 1971.

Nicholson, Helen. *A Brief History of the Knights Templar*. London: Constable and Robinson, 2010.

Noyes, Alfred. *The Early Romances of William Morris*. London: Dent and Sons, 1907.

Open University, The. "Fenner Brockway." Making Britain, n.d. https://www.open.ac.uk/researchprojects/makingbritain/content/fenner-brockway.

Powell, W. Raymond. *Keir Hardie in West Ham*. London: Socialist History Society, 2004.

"Preacher Turns Socialist." *New York Times*, Aug. 1, 1907.

Pugh, Martin. *Speak for Britain! A New History of the Labour Party*. London: Vintage, 2011.

Reid, Fred. *Keir Hardie: The Making of a Socialist*. London: Croom Helm Limited, 1978.

"Religion and Labour. Mr Keir Hardie's Views." *Western Daily Mercury*, Apr. 6, 1912.

"Religion and the Labour Movement." *Sheffield Independent*, Jan. 16, 1915.

Renan, Ernest. *The Life of Jesus*. London: Dent and Sons, 1927. First published 1863.

———. "What Is a Nation?" Cooper, Mar. 11, 1882. https://web.archive.org/web/20110827065548/http://www.cooper.edu/humanities/core/hss3/e_renan.html.

Ruskin, John. "Unto This Last." In *The Works of John Ruskin*, edited by E. T. Cook and Alexander Wedderburn, 17:25–114. London: Allen, 1905.

Scribner, Robert W. *The German Reformation*. London: Macmillan, 1986.

Spargo, John. *Karl Marx: His Life and Work*. New York: Huebsch, 1912.

Stabel, Peter. "Guilds in Late Medieval Flanders: Myths and Realities of Guild Life in an Export-Orientated Environment." *Journal of Medieval History* 30 (2004) 187–212.

Stewart, William. *J. Keir Hardie: A Biography*. Westport, CT: Greenwood: 1970. First published 1921.

Ten Labour Members of Parliament and of Other Bodies. *Labour and Religion*. Delhi: Pranava, 2018. First published 1910.

Thompson, Laurence. *The Enthusiasts: A Biography of John and Katharine Bruce Glasier*. London: Gollancz, 1971.

Tisdall, Simon. "Europe's Lurch to the Right Rolls On." *Guardian Weekly*, June 9, 2023.

Tracey, Herbert, ed. *The Book of the Labour Party: Its History, Growth, Policy and Leaders*. 3 vols. London: Caxton, 1925.

Trevor, John, ed. *Labour Church Hymn Book*. Manchester, UK: Labour Church Institute, 1892.

United Nations. "Refugees and Migrants: A Crisis of Solidarity." United Nations, n.d. https://www.un.org/en/academic-impact/refugees-and-migrants-crisis-solidarity#:~:text=But%20this%20is%20not%20a,ease%20and%20 resolve%20their%20plight.

Watson, Robert A. "Mr Keir Hardie on Socialism." *Southland Times*, Mar. 31, 1894.

Wheen, Francis. *Karl Marx*. London: Fourth Estate, 1999.

Whitman, Walt. *The Complete Poems*. London: Penguin, 1977.

Williams, Anthony Alan John. "Christian Socialism as Political Ideology." PhD diss., University of Liverpool, 2016.

Williams, Francis. *Fifty Years' March: The Rise of the Labour Party*. London: Odhams, 1950.

Wilson, Les, dir. *Inside the Mind of Robert Burns*. BBC Scotland, first broadcast Jan. 21, 2020.

Winstanley, Gerrard. *A Common Treasury*. London: Verso, 2011.

Working Class Movement's Library. "Keir Hardie Centenary Conference." Independent Labour, Sept. 26, 2015. https://www.independentlabour.org. uk/2015/09/18/keir-hardie-centenary-.

Wright, Tony. *Socialisms: Old and New*. London: Routledge, 1996.

Wrigley, Chris. "The ILP and the Second International: The Early Years, 1893–1905." In *The Centennial History of the Independent Labour Party*, edited by David James et al., 299–314. Halifax, UK: Ryburn Academic, 1992.

Index

Printed in Great Britain
by Amazon

35522642R00066